Harambee!

The Prime Minister of Kenya's Speeches 1963-1964

FROM THE ATTAINMENT OF
INTERNAL SELF-GOVERNMENT TO THE
THRESHOLD OF THE KENYA REPUBLIC

Jomo Kenyatta

Foreword by the Rt. Hon. Malcolm MacDonald,
Governor-General of Kenya

The Text edited and arranged by Anthony Cullen
on instructions of the Permanent Secretary,
Prime Minister's Office

Nairobi

OXFORD UNIVERSITY PRESS

London · New York

1964

Oxford University Press, Amen House, London E.C.4
GLASGOW NEW YORK TORONTO MELBOURNE WELLINGTON
BOMBAY CALCUTTA MADRAS KARACHI LAHORE DACCA
CAPE TOWN SALISBURY NAIROBI IBADAN ACCRA
KUALA LUMPUR HONG KONG

Cover design by
HILLARY R. CORREIA

Printed and bound in Nairobi by
East African Printers, Kenya, Ltd.

Contents

Contents

Plates

Mzee Jomo Kenyatta, first and only Prime Minister of Kenya, first President of the Kenya Republic, pictured at his Gatundu home.

(Appearing between pages 52—53)

1—Mzee Kenyatta being sworn in as Kenya's first Prime Minister on Internal Self-government Day.

2—The Prime Minister garlanded by young girls during an early official visit to Nakuru.

3—Jomo Kenyatta addressing an impromptu meeting while on tour in the Western Region.

4—The Prime Minister watching elephant at Kilaguni when on his way back from the Coast.

5—Mzee Jomo Kenyatta holding aloft the Constitutional Instruments in the Stadium on Uhuru Day.

6—The Prime Minister receiving the Freedom of the City of Nairobi from Mayor Rubia.

7—Mzee Kenyatta with the members of his Cabinet and some senior officials following Independence.

8—The Prime Minister at the Academic Ceremony where he was elected an Honorary Fellow.

9—Jomo Kenyatta listening to the Kenya Rifles band playing the revised National Anthem.

10—The Prime Minister on a tour of cattle exhibits at the Elgeyo-Marakwet County Show, in the Rift Valley.

11—Mzee Jomo Kenyatta being decorated by the Emperor Haile Selassie with the Distinguished Order of the Queen of Sheba at State House in Nairobi.

All photographs have been supplied by the Kenya Department of Information

Foreword

by the Rt. Hon. MALCOLM MACDONALD

The speeches of Mzee Jomo Kenyatta published in this book have been the inspiration of the young Kenyan nation. Two years ago few people—either African, Asian or European inside Kenya, or of any race outside it—thought that the new nation could be successfully born in 1963; and many others who supposed that its birth soon afterwards was inevitable assumed that it would be still-born, or that within a few months of its emergence from the womb of Mother Africa it would die from chronic internal disorders.

Now this book is being published on Independent Kenya's first birthday; and the infant nation is hale and hearty, with every prospect of enjoying very many Happy Returns of the Day.

The man responsible for making the seemingly impossible become possible is Jomo Kenyatta. Of course a share of the credit belongs to others also—to his team of Ministers, who are showing notable industry, ability and judgement in conducting Government policy; to the African population in general, whose grand qualities of good sense and friendliness have responded to their leader's appeal for 'Harambee!'; and to the members of the European and Asian communities who have accepted the new regime with sincere loyalty.

But Jomo Kenyatta is responsible for enabling them all to co-operate together in constructive ways. Without his strong, wise, unifying leadership they might easily have fallen apart in fratricidal inter-tribal, inter-racial or inter-class bickerings, with disastrous results for the nation. That was very possible so soon after the bitter emotional stresses and strains of the recent past, with its white Colonial domination, its tragic Mau Mau episode, and other taut situations—not to mention the deep-rooted tribal rivalries of an earlier African age. One of the marks of Kenyatta's genius as an orator and statesman was his choice of the motto for the new state on the day when it became independent. Until then the universal cry of the African nationalists in Kenya had been 'Uhuru', meaning 'Freedom'; but now he declared that the national slogan must be 'Harambee', meaning 'Let's all pull together'. He emphasized that national freedom had been won; that it had never been an end in itself, but only a great means to a greater end; that the ultimate aim was a harmonious and prosperous Kenyan nation;

and that such a nation could only be built by a hard, co-operative effort by Kenyans of every tribe and community. His choice of the word 'Harambee' was racey of the African soil. It is the oft-repeated refrain chanted by East African labourers as they pull heavily laden carts, or perform other strenuous manual tasks which require a united effort by a team of workers. Kenyatta's shouted proclamation of it in his gay, authoritative voice as he waved his famous fly whisk—which he wields like the sceptre of a king—at the assembled multitudes on Independence Day had an electrifying effect in summoning the nation to its fresh duties.

The adoption of that motto reflected one of Kenyatta's fine qualities: his capacity to view the past as something that is finished —the lessons of which should never be forgotten, but which otherwise should be dismissed to its proper place in history, whilst everyone turns their attention to the new, challenging problems of the present and the future. Many a victorious Nationalist leader would have been tempted in the hour of his triumph to dwell on the past struggle, to recall its hostilities and bitternesses, to chide the now vanquished opponents, and to revive the emotions of those times in the breasts of his followers, so as to emphasize his own position as a successful champion. But Kenyatta's head is too wise and his heart too big for any stooping to those tactics. He knew that such an attitude would prejudice Kenya's future by promoting a wrong, backward-looking instead of forward-looking mood in the masses of his African followers, by recalling and encouraging old inter-tribal differences of opinion, and by arousing feelings of insecurity among the European and Asian people whose co-operation would be essential. And so—with courage in the face of possible criticism by lesser men—he preached the doctrine of forgetting the past, concentrating on the problems of the present, and striving for the aims of the future.

The speeches and writings published in this book are packed with his thoughts on those problems and aims. They speak for themselves with an eloquence which needs no embroidery from me or anyone else. Nor is this brief Foreword the place in which to attempt a full-length appreciation of their great author. I shall only say here that Jomo Kenyatta's clear vision, unshakeable steadfastness, indomitable courage, ripe wisdom and compassionate humanity, combined with his magnetic popular appeal, make him one of the supreme statesmen of our time.

Introduction

The content of this volume is an edited presentation of approximately one hundred speeches, delivered by Mzee Jomo Kenyatta during his tenure of office as the first and only Prime Minister of Kenya.

The period covered—nearly eighteen months—extends from the attainment of Internal Self-government in June, 1963, to the threshold of the Kenya Republic.

Published in December, 1964, on the first anniversary of Kenya's Independence, this book will mark the formal institution of the Kenya Republic, with Jomo Kenyatta as President.

Edited presentation does not imply any amendment to the public record. The phrase relates simply to arrangement. Chronological order and verbatim reproduction could have led only to confusion. Material contained in the speeches themselves has thus been presented under a dozen different subject headings. Some speeches appear in full; others have been split into subject components. No speech has been paraphrased; some have been condensed.

Introductory or qualifying matter—in small type throughout the book—serves merely to transform into narrative a series of speeches that, without such aid, would lack identity and perspective.

This book conveys the philosophy and the purpose of Mzee Kenyatta during a critical era: his work to build Kenya; his striving for unity in Africa; his projection of Africa in world society.

1

'The Fruits of Life'

ON October the 20th, 1964, celebrated throughout Kenya as Kenyatta Day, the Prime Minister delivered—over radio and television—a special Address to the Nation. In this, he summed up the policies and achievements of his Government during ten months of Independence, and he outlined to the people something of his philosophy as a man. This speech marks the end-point of this contemporary record, of the contribution made by Mzee Jomo Kenyatta—in dynamic thinking and untiring effort—to the building of Kenya, and to the new place of Africa in a shrinking world:

On this Day that bears my name, I want to speak to you all without formality, in your homes or in community centres or wherever you might be. And I want to speak to you all, today, not just as a Prime Minister, but as a man. For although—by your wish—I am the leader of my country, the recollection of this Day in all your hearts and minds means more than just a tribute to a title. It reaches back in time. And it reminds me very vividly of all the phases and milestones of more than forty years of work and service, dedicated to the freedom and the dignity of Africa, and to pan-African ideals.

This is the first celebration of Kenyatta Day since, here in Kenya, our struggle for Uhuru was ended, and we became an independent sovereign State. I am proud to think back on the part that I played in this struggle. Much was direct contribution. But it gladdened me to know, through a long period of anxieties and sufferings, that my conception of duty—to this country and its people—inspired and upheld others, when I could not be there.

Our struggle was a just one. All the noble Charters and Declarations of history, and all the Constitutions that enshrine human rights, have sprung from one paramount truth: that men in their spirit and in their striving, under the law, have the right to be free. The world in these past years has moved rapidly forward, from the Colonial age. Peoples in many continents have been freed, and not just from political bondage. Their talents and their ambitions and their cultures have all been released. Their productive energies have altered the old pattern of economic privilege. Their philosophies have made impact on the thinking of mankind, bringing fresh hope to the cause of world peace.

All this is what we sought for ourselves. And on this Day I share your joy that we in Kenya have the rights and the responsibilities of free men. To me, this is a monument to years of service.

What I want to say to you now is what these years have taught me. Triumph in a struggle of this kind cannot be achieved without a long history of setbacks and sufferings, of failure and humiliation. But all this is worthwhile, and all can be forgotten, when its outcome is the foundation on which a future can be built. It is the future, my friends, that is living, and the past that is dead. In all that I have seen, in many countries and at many periods of my life, never has there seemed any purpose in arguments about the past, or any nobility in motives of revenge.

There have been murmurs here in Kenya about the part played by one set of people, or another set of people, in the struggle for Uhuru. There has been talk of the contribution made, or refused, by this group or that. There has been—at times—vindictive comment, and a finger of scorn has been pointed at some selected race, or group, or tribe. All this is unworthy of our future here.

I want this celebration of Kenyatta Day to mean more to you all than just some particular Tuesday in the calendar. Let this be the day on which all of us commit ourselves to erase from our minds all the hatreds and the difficulties of those years which now belong to history. Let us agree that we shall never refer to the past. Let us instead unite, in all our utterances and activities, in concern for the reconstruction of our country and the vitality of Kenya's future.

How our future must be built here was outlined to you first in the KANU Election Manifesto. This was our blueprint, still valid today. And whenever I consult this Party statement, I am struck afresh by the vision of its approach, and the wisdom of its declarations, on the issues that mean everything to you all.

As this Manifesto made clear, achievement of sovereign status and the urge for reform must have a fundamental purpose, that is never set aside. This is to remove from our people the burden of poverty, the scourge of malnutrition and ill-health, the frustration of illiteracy, and the demoralizing lack of economic opportunity.

Here is our motive, in all that we are working on now. Some of you have wondered if I and the Party had forgotten all these fundamental needs. But let me assure you today that I and my Government will never rest until victory over all these evils and injustices is finally won.

I know that all of you—the unemployed; farmers and business-men; workers and students and public servants; the parents of our children—had high expectations on our Independence Day. This feeling serves the country well. We need to maintain the sense and the spirit of ambition and urgency, in all our social and economic affairs. But if you perhaps have been feeling that we might have moved faster than we have, just remember certain things:

Kenya has been an independent sovereign State for only ten months of one year. However hard we worked in this opening stage of nation building, and even with the assistance of miracles, it would be impossible to eliminate all past imperfections and injustices, and to meet all modern aspirations and needs, in such a short time. But a great deal has in fact been done.

Through our programme of Africanization, we have done much to augment the status and security of our country. Nearly all the high appointments in the Civil Service are now held by Africans. In the Police force, this process will shortly extend to the rank of Inspector-General. The Kenya Army will soon be commanded by an African, and many other African Officers—up to the rank of Lieutenant-Colonel—have successfully completed training to take their rightful place. We have founded the Kenya Air Force, and a Kenya Navy will be formally established before long.

While on this subject, I want to emphasize here one point that I have made before. The purpose of our Africanization programme is simple enough: to maintain an efficient and effective machine of Government by and for Kenya's people. Any breakdown in the machinery of Government, at any level, would not carry the country forward, but would cast us back. For this reason, Africanization has not been, and cannot be, an automatic programme based on colour or race. We need at many levels not only talent and loyalty, but also experience. This is why training schemes have been insti-ted, and must be continued, to equip our people for posts of high responsibility, and give them opportunity to gain the maturity that comes from experience.

I have made it clear many times that our Government will not discriminate against any citizens on matters of employment opportunity, recruitment and promotion. All citizens of Kenya, regardless of their race or colour or country of origin, have equal opportunities and duties in the building of our Public Service. I expect all civil servants—including those who have become Kenya citizens—to work loyally for the country.

At present, the loyalty and experience of many expatriate Officers are serving a critical need. We shall have to recruit more expatriate Officers, technicians and professional men, if the country is to progress rapidly in fulfilment of the Development Plan. It is most important that these Officers be made to feel welcome here, and be assured that the job they are doing for Kenya is appreciated. I must therefore urge some political leaders, and some Members of our National Assembly, to bear this in mind. They should refrain from making any statements likely to undermine the spirit and confidence of these expatriate Officers, now and for some time ahead.

Within this short period of ten months, our six-year Development Plan has been prepared and published, and work has already started to build a new economic and social fabric to meet the hopes and serve the wellbeing of all Kenya's people. We have in fact recorded economic progress—actual and pending—on a very significant scale, aided in many cases by investment in concrete projects, or development loans, from overseas. The oil refinery, and new textile factories, and new industries of many kinds, are there for all to see. In addition, some massive agricultural developments have been introduced or planned, involving—for example—the greatly increased production of sugar, and of cotton on irrigation schemes, and of tea. Experts are now studying ways to expand our livestock industries. We are welcoming visitors from many countries of the world, and have developed tourism, through the conservation of natural resources, as a major enterprise.

The Education Commission, appointed early this year, will be reporting soon, as a vital step on the road towards our eventual goal of free, compulsory education for all. The Development Plan itself provided that priority should be given to secondary education, as a means of serving our future needs for skilled manpower in fields of science and technology.

As the background to all this, more than sixty thousand of our people have now been accommodated on the settlement schemes.

We already have in being more than a hundred co-operative farms. Jobs have been found for tens of thousands of the unemployed, through the Tripartite Agreement and on Government-sponsored projects. Thousands of our young men have been taken into the security forces, or been given new hope by means of training schemes, within the whole inspiration of the National Youth Service.

In the political field, we have decided and arranged that Kenya shall become a Republic on December the 12th. During this very week, full details of the new Republican Constitution will be placed before Parliament and the country. We have actively pursued the cause of greater unity within East Africa, and I am proud to reaffirm here and now that Kenya has played a prominent part throughout this year in the purposes and active work of the Organization of African Unity. In foreign affairs, and in all our dealings with the countries of the world, our policy has been that of non-alignment, and this we have maintained without any of the damage to our sovereignty or dignity or economic interests that some observers had predicted.

We are grateful to our friends—both in the West and in the East—for their generous response to requests for assistance and proposals for co-operation. In this vital initial year of Independence, this has helped to fulfil our commitments and launch our new plans.

But I must warn the country now that, in the long term, the prosperity and development of Kenya will depend on the efforts of the people themselves. We must work hard and constantly towards the greatest possible degree of self-reliance. We cannot and must not always rely on outside aid. It is not good for the economy, or for the morale of a country, to be greatly dependent on overseas assistance, which itself may be influenced by changes in policy or personnel. We have accepted the kind of foreign aid that is without strings. But at the same time, there are always subtle obligations. Kenya must develop her own strength. And we must be in a position as well to help others, our brothers elsewhere in Africa, with continuing struggles for freedom and economic independence.

I have told you enough, I think, to show that the attainment of our Independence has been followed by the dynamic and properly-planned activity of your Government. But just before I close, let me re-emphasize some important ideas and beliefs:

What is in my mind now—and what should be in the minds of all of you—is to look forward, not to look back. Our children may learn about heroes of the past. Our task is to make ourselves architects of their future. And in this, we must think beyond self. I would be satisfied now, with my life, simply through knowing that I had made some contribution to a free and better life for Kenya's people. I would be satisfied even if I were not Prime Minister, with many grave tasks and responsibilities still lying ahead.

The fruits of life, my friends, are there, for as long as one has the strength to seek them. I say to you now that service to one's fellow men can never be confined by a price or a reward. Its true satisfaction comes in the nature of dedication. In my long life, this has been dedication to my country and its people, to the cause of freedom and pan-African ideals, to progress through unity and the bounty of our land.

Not all of you can be leaders. But all of you have your families, your farms or businesses, your daily tasks. By applying all that you are and all that you do to the cause of national unity and the progress of our country, then this dedication which I have known and enjoyed will be something we all can share.

2

Dawn of the Republic

THE starting-point of this record, of the contemporary scene, fell on June the 1st, 1963, when Kenya attained Internal Self-government. In a brief speech at the swearing-in ceremony outside the Prime Minister's Office in Nairobi, Jomo Kenyatta first publicly voiced what has since become the national motto and rallying-cry . . . all pull together . . . HARAMBEE!

This is one of the happiest moments of my life. We are now embarking on the final brief stage which will lead this country to Independence. It is not a celebration by one Party as its Election victory. Rather must it be a rejoicing of all the people of this land at the progress towards the goal of Independence.

But as we celebrate, let us remember that constitutional advance is not the greatest end in itself. Many of our people suffer in sickness. Many are poor beyond endurance. Too many live out narrow lives beneath a burden of ignorance. As we participate in pomp and circumstance, and as we make merry at this time, remember this: we are relaxing before the toil that is to come. We must work harder to fight our enemies—ignorance, sickness and poverty.

I therefore give you the call: HARAMBEE! Let us all work hard together for our country, Kenya.

TWO evenings later, in the course of a broadcast message to the whole country, the Prime Minister ushered in the new nation-building phase, urging the country to create what he called a 'sense of national direction and identity':

Following the swearing-in of the new Cabinet on Saturday, we now have the team which is going to lead Kenya to independence.

I do not want to discuss the details of the policies we shall implement. You will already have heard much about this in our speeches, broadcasts and various statements. But I would like to remind you of some of the principles which underlie the programme we intend to carry out.

First, I must point out that the Government now in power is the Government for the whole of Kenya. It is not just for those who elected us. We shall care equally for those people who gave us their votes, and those who did not. All those who do not agree with us have proper ways of making their views known. The Opposition is formally recognized in our national Constitution, and can play a constructive role in nation-building. On the other hand, we shall be as firm as any other Government in dealing with anyone who turns to subversive action.

I believe firmly that, if this country of ours is to prosper, we must create a sense of togetherness, of national familyhood. In Swahili, we express this by the word 'ujamaa', which can also be roughly translated as socialism.

We must bring all the communities of Kenya together, to build a unified nation. In this task, we shall make use of those attitudes of self-help, good-neighbourliness and communal assistance, which are such an important feature of our traditional societies.

Where there has been racial hatred, it must be ended. Where there has been tribal animosity, it will be finished. Let us not dwell upon the bitterness of the past. I would rather look to the future, to the good new Kenya, not to the bad old days. If we can create this sense of national direction and identity, we shall have gone a long way towards solving our economic problems.

We hold out no empty promises of achieving Utopia overnight. What we hold out to every citizen is the prospect of hard work, justly rewarded.

THE theme of national unity, as the principal ingredient of effective and prosperous nationhood, is one that Mzee Kenyatta has constantly pursued, from the moment of Internal Self-government to the dawn of the Kenya Republic. These quotations will illustrate his thinking, and the substance of his appeal. In Parliament, first in July, 1963, and then in June, 1964, he said this:

I would beseech the Opposition to realize that we have a country to build, that we have a nation to build, and that we cannot develop by throwing mud in one another's faces. They should recognize the Government and work with it harmoniously. We want the people of Kenya to work as one and to work for the sake of Kenya, for the benefit and progress of all the people and not for one small section . . . . Whether people are KANU or KADU, and no matter to what tribe they belong, the Government knows only citizens.

Development money will be allocated according to the needs of any part of Kenya.

*   *   *

We have reached a stage where we must keep the confidence which we have created. Unless we maintain confidence, people will get jittery. People will be afraid of bringing their money here if they see that we are not united, and then we would be without business.

I say to everyone that we should work together—KANU and KADU should work together—so that we can build a new nation, a strong nation, and have a prosperous country, rather than grumbling amongst ourselves and hearing Members in the House saying that the Government is doing nothing.

We are working hard, not for the sake of individuals, nor for the sake of self, but for the country as a whole.

THEN, in addresses to two mass political rallies in Nairobi, both during June, 1964:

If we were not united, we could not have achieved all this. If there is tribalism and racialism, it will impede our progress. You should support the Government which you have elected. If we stand shoulder to shoulder in our struggle, we shall overcome our enemies: poverty, ignorance and disease.

*   *   *

Do not think Kenyatta is doing all this alone, by himself. He is doing everything in concert with your Government. With your co-operation, the Government will build a new Kenya . . . . I beg you with all my heart to join together. Those who spread false gossip should be accursed.

WIDER afield, during speeches in the Mombasa Stadium (February, 1964), to the Meru Co-operative Union (August, 1964), and to a political rally at Githunguri (September, 1964), the Prime Minister said:

Brothers and countrymen: thank you for welcoming us in this part of the country. We have indeed been welcomed by all the people . . . . Now that we have attained our independence, unity must be our theme. You asked me to rule, and I shall rule well. Whoever offers challenge will know that this Government has the mandate of the people.

* * *

Unless the country can help itself, then it cannot develop. We must make systematic efforts to harness the spirit of self-help, and of national unity.

* * *

To you now I say: let us unite and fight for the future of this country, fight the battle of eliminating poverty among our people. In this we must join in a holy alliance. No other union is greater than the alliance of humanity . . . . There are those who say: 'we are big; Kenyatta is our Prime Minister', just as though I were a Kikuyu Prime Minister. But for every intent and purpose, I am not just a Prime Minister for the Kikuyu. Whether you are a Kikuyu, or a member of another tribe, is beside the point. My work is essentially for the African people, and I have no room for tribalists in my heart.

THE same pattern of inspiration was heard in the course of 'barazas' held by Mzee Jomo Kenyatta with the Masai (June, 1964), first at Kajiado and then at Narok:

It is my wish to demonstrate to you that the Africans of this country are now free. The period of European rule is past. We are now all citizens of this country. Since we Africans are ruling our country, all of us should rule it together, because if we are not united we shall not be strong. The Masai are one people with us.

* * *

Now the reporters can see that these 10,000 people at Narok . . . (Masailand) . . . have demonstrated their confidence in the Government.

THERE was a constant theme—united effort; peaceful reconstruction—going back to one of the first big public meetings addressed by Mzee as Prime Minister. This was at Ol Kalou in August, 1963:

Without unity, we cannot do anything worthwhile . . . . We want the world to know that Kenya can rule itself. By learning to respect one another, and working together, we can give an example to Africa and the world of how people of different origins can come together—as citizens of one country—to build a peaceful nation.

BUT the creation of national unity—alone—could be little more than the essential background, throughout this period, to all the practical negotiations and legal mechanics of constitutional advancement and change. On July the 2nd, 1963, speaking in Parliament just a month after his swearing-in, the Prime Minister launched the country on a new era in this context, by announcing the date for Kenya's Independence:

Today, I shall announce to the House and to the country the date for Kenya's full Independence, in other words the date when our struggle against Colonialism ends permanently.

During the Election campaign, my Party promised the country full Independence as soon as possible within 1963.

In the first week of our Government, we sent a message to the United Kingdom Government asking for a meeting with the Secretary of State, to discuss the next steps in Kenya's movement towards Independence. On June the 14th, a Ministerial delegation led by the Minister for Justice and Constitutional Affairs, Mr. Mboya . . . (and including the Minister of State in the Prime Minister's Office, Mr. Murumbi; the Minister for Pan African Affairs, Mr. Koinange; and the Attorney-General, Mr. Njonjo) . . . left for London. This delegation held talks with the Secretary of State for the Colonies and Commonwealth Affairs, and returned to Kenya on June the 25th.

I am glad and proud to be able to tell the House and the country that this delegation was a tremendous success.

Mr. Sandys agreed to convene a Conference in London towards the end of September, the purpose of which would be to settle the final form of Kenya's Constitution. Representatives of the Government and Opposition in the Legislature, and of the European community, will be invited to attend. In order to facilitate the work of the Conference, preparatory discussions will be held in Nairobi.

Having regard to the date envisaged for the inauguration of the East African Federation, and subject to the necessary steps being completed in time, Kenya will become Independent on December the 12th.

I know that the House will wish to join me in extending my Government's appreciation to Mr. Sandys, for his co-operation and understanding in dealing with our efforts to achieve Independence within 1963.

AND it was in this same speech in the House that Jomo Kenyatta offered what he described as 'a word of advice', to members of the parliamentary Opposition:

We in the Government accept fully our responsibilities, but that is not enough unless that spirit in the Government is supported by a similar spirit and resolution on the part of all Members of this House and the public at large.

I would like to point out here that we have recognized the rights of the Opposition, but I am rather worried that the Opposition is increasingly tending to fail to appreciate its responsibilities and duties to Kenya. There is emerging a tendency towards 'opposition for the sake of opposition'. Negative and destructive opposition can only do harm to democracy, and—what is more—it can quickly lead to the destruction of the privileges and rights of the Opposition itself.

This is not a threat, but a word of advice. We will accept fair and constructive criticism, but the country cannot afford the luxury of negative and destructive opposition.

Let us move forward in the spirit of 'harambee'. Let us move forward in the spirit of unity, co-operation and hard work.

DURING the little more than six months that separated Internal Self-government from Independence, there was the final Constitutional Conference convened by the British Government in London. On the eve of his departure from Nairobi at the head of the Kenya Government's delegation—September the 21st, 1963—Jomo Kenyatta used these words:

Since the Election and the formation of an African Government, I and my Ministers have spared no effort in our endeavours to create unity and understanding throughout the country. The Government appreciates the response of the people to this call, and we have been very impressed with the way the ordinary man in Kenya has been keen to serve his country, and is not committed to tribalism or secession.

At the same time, the Government understands the fears and anxieties of some communities, and hopes that—by its example during these few months in office—such fears will be seen to be unfounded. The KANU Government is concerned with the welfare of all the people, regardless of their race or tribe, and this will be the policy of the Government in the future.

The final talks on the Constitution are to be held in London next week. The Government is pleased to see that the Opposition has at last decided to attend the talks.

In presenting its case, the Government will be guided by the wishes of the people, which have been so clearly demonstrated in the General Election, as well as in the County Council and Municipal elections. Our purpose is to establish a strong and effective Government, and to promote unity rather than encourage disintegration.

The Kenya Government delegation will urge on the British Government the need for a Constitution for Kenya that is both realistic and workable. It will press for a Constitution that is based not on fear and suspicion, but on faith and confidence in Kenya. The assumption of faith and good intentions on the part of all groups and communities within Kenya, rather than of hostility and conflict of interests, must be the starting-point for a peaceful and united Kenya.

Before our departure for London, I wish to take this opportunity to appeal to all the people of Kenya to keep calm and maintain the peace. The new era that Kenya will enter as an Independent nation—in the spirit of 'harambee'—in December, is one which will call for dedication, hard work and unity. This is the challenge of the future.

JUST a month later—October the 20th, 1963—the Prime Minister arrived back in Nairobi, and reported to the country on the outcome of this constitutional mission:

Four weeks ago, we went to London for the final Constitutional Conference before Kenya's Independence. It has been four weeks of hard bargaining, but I am glad to say that all has ended well. I can now confirm that the date for our Independence will definitely be December the 12th. This is only 51 days ahead.

I hope that, now that we are back with this confirmation, anxieties will disappear, and all our people will instead concentrate on readiness for Uhuru celebrations. Uhuru has been long awaited, both at home and abroad, and will attract a lot of interest. I am determined that it shall be a day to remember for all our people for all time.

In addition to confirming the date for Independence, we have been able to secure a number of significant changes to the Constitution. These include amendments to create one Public Service Commission of Kenya instead of eight; a unified control and command of the entire Police force; and a change in the amendment machinery to enable changes to take place on a two-thirds national referendum.

The whole purpose of the Government was to secure a flexible and workable Constitution for Kenya. I assure the country that the new Constitution now provides a strong base for a united Kenya nation, within which everyone—regardless of tribe or race—shall feel safe and secure. Within this State, there will be no room for domination, but there will be ample room for everyone to participate and contribute towards our efforts for nation building.

There is no room for autonomy or secession. Such talk is idle, and will lead nowhere. Why should anyone deny the Kalenjin, Masai or Coastal tribes the right to be part of the new Kenya nation? Why should anyone try to deny these tribes the right to participate in and contribute towards the exciting task of creating a new nation? These are questions which I am sure the people will soon ask of their leaders. I have no hesitation in saying that the people will reject petty and negative leadership.

I know that one of the most sensitive questions in our country is land. This has been played on by some people. I now give a categorical assurance that, under the Constitution, all tribal land is entrenched in the tribal authority, and no one can take away land belonging to another tribe.

I do not regard our mission to London as a victory for KANU. This is a victory for Kenya, and for responsible and sensible policies aimed at the welfare of all our people. Let us not talk of Opposition and Government. Let us talk of Kenya and our people's need. I invite the Opposition leaders to forget the past, and come together with us to form a united front to fight our real enemies—poverty, ignorance and disease.

All of us want to fight these three evils. So why do we not join together now—in the spirit of 'harambee'—and move forward?

I see no shame in forgetting the past. To do this is an act of wisdom and courage that goes with genuine leadership. Here is our opportunity: let it never be said that we refused to take it.

THEN followed Uhuru. A crowded week of pageant and ceremony that Kenya will never forget was symbolized—one midnight in the Uhuru Stadium—by the unfurling of the Kenya flag. But beneath the symbols of Independence lay the more serious trappings of history. As the leading architect of Kenya's freedom, Mzee Jomo Kenyatta was the central figure of this period. But shoulders which carried the triumph of freedom now bore—as well—the responsibilities of nationhood. On Uhuru Day itself—December the 12th, 1963—the Prime Minister received the constitutional instruments of Independence. This was his reply:

Your Royal Highness, Your Excellency, distinguished guests, ladies and gentlemen . . . .

It is with great pride and pleasure that I receive these constitutional instruments today as the embodiment of Kenya's freedom. This is the greatest day in Kenya's history, and the happiest day of my life.

Our march to freedom has been long and difficult. There have been times of despair, when only the burning conviction of the rightness of our cause has sustained us. Today, the tragedies and misunderstandings of the past are behind us. Today, we start on the great adventure of building the Kenya nation.

As we start on this great task, it is right that we who are assembled at this historic ceremony here today, and all the people of Kenya, should remember and pay tribute to those people of all races, tribes and colours who—over the years—have made their contribution to Kenya's rich heritage: administrators, farmers, missionaries, traders and others, and above all the people of Kenya themselves. All have laboured to make this fair land of Kenya the thriving country it is today. It behoves each one of us to vow that, in the days ahead, we shall be worthy of our great inheritance.

Your Royal Highness, your presence here today as the personal representative of Her Majesty the Queen is for us a great honour, and one which gives the highest pleasure to all the people of Kenya. We thank Her Majesty for her message of good wishes, and would request you, Sir, to convey to the Queen the warm greetings of all our people.

We welcome also today Her Majesty's Secretary of State for Commonwealth Relations, who has been so closely concerned with us in the final stages of our march to Independence. With Britain, which has watched over our destinies for so long, we now enter a new relationship. The close ties which have bound our two countries are not severed today. Rather, they will now grow in strength as we work together as two sovereign nations within the Commonwealth, that unique association of free and independent States to whose counsels we look forward to making our contribution.

To all our honoured guests, I extend—on behalf of the people of Kenya—a warm and fraternal welcome to our country on this great occasion. Your presence here today brings added pleasure to our rejoicings.

Today is rightly a day of great rejoicing. But it must also be a day of dedication. Freedom is a right, and without it the dignity of man is violated. But freedom by itself is not enough. At home, we have a duty to ensure that all our citizens are delivered from the afflictions of poverty, ignorance and disease, otherwise freedom for many of our people will be neither complete nor meaningful. We shall count as our friends, and welcome as fellow-citizens, every man, woman and child in Kenya—regardless of race, tribe, colour or creed—who is ready to help us in this great task of advancing the social wellbeing of all our people.

Freedom also means that we are now a member of the international community, and that we have a duty to work for the peace of the world. Abroad, we shall count as our friends all those who strive for peace.

My friends, we are now an independent nation, and our destiny is henceforward in our own hands. I call on every Kenyan to join me today in this great adventure of nation building. In the spirit of 'harambee', let us all work together so to mould our country that it will set an example to the world in progress, toleration and high endeavour.

A ND then, after completing delivery of his formal speech, Jomo Kenyatta paused for a moment, and put his papers down. He gazed around at the huge crowds thronging the Uhuru Stadium, and remembering—as is typical of him—that this was their moment of history as well as his, he began to speak to the people, in Kiswahili. He spoke to the people and held them in his hand, using the art of mirth at times to break the strain of attention, drawing frequent agreement and acclaim. The people did not simply listen: they became part of the image he created. There was none of the posturing of those who rule by force or fear. This was just expression of the rarely-penetrated mystery of leadership. He said:

We are all grateful for the greetings from Her Majesty the Queen which the Duke of Edinburgh has read to us today. We ask him—when he returns to Britain—to convey our greetings to the Queen: tell her that, although we have become independent, we shall still remain her friends. I think, my brothers, that our friendship with the Queen and the Government of the United Kingdom will now be of greater value. Before, this was not of our choice; it was being forced upon us. But now, although we have broken all chains, this friendship can be real and of great importance.

I also want to thank the Duke of Edinburgh for having brought us an important book, different from any other. This book says that all the people of Kenya are free, that the people of Kenya are up-holding their own Government, whether anyone else likes it or not. We thank the Duke of Edinburgh again, and we shall never forget that it was he who brought us this important book.

I am grateful that distinguished guests from all over the world have joined us in celebrating the achievement of Independence for our country. I greet you on behalf of the people of Kenya. We all wish you a happy and enjoyable stay in our country. But, as you know, mistakes and imperfections can be found here and there, and should you encounter such things—be you black, white or brown—we ask you to excuse us and accept that this is unintentional. We are all human, and human beings are sometimes bound to make mistakes.

What I have to say now is for the people of this country, but first let me say a word to our brothers in Africa who broke the chains of Colonialism before us. I say to them: we are now in-dependent after you. You have already tasted the honey of Uhuru, and now that we are with you, I know that this is very sweet.

But to all who have Independence, I say: this would be meaning-less if, in our Africa, some of our brothers are still under the yoke of Colonialism. We therefore face a great challenge, to help those of our brothers who are left behind, still dominated by foreign rule. If we look at South Africa, and if we look at Mozambique and Angola, we find our brothers still being exploited. It is thus our duty to fight, by all means available to us, so that our brothers can achieve their Independence.

African unity is very important. If there is no unity in the whole of Africa, we shall still be slaves: we shall have entered into a new type of slavery, the slavery of divide-and-rule by more powerful countries which have tasted the sweetness of ruling, and which—whether waking or sleeping—only think of ruling Africa. And when they sleep, a dream comes to them urging them to divide Africa, divide and then rule. It is our duty to stop this, and the only means is unity, working together.

If we achieve unity, the whole world will respect us. We shall be the foundation and the shield of mother Africa. Our Africa has been milked until she is almost dry. Now we want to restore and sustain mother Africa, so we can enjoy the little milk that is left. If we do not do this, we will be finished. I want to emphasize that our salvation will be brought about by unity.

Some people may say that—alas!—Kenyatta now is advocating a colour-bar. This is not so; I have no colour feelings at all. What I want is for us to be united, so we can go forward and co-operate with the rest of the world. This is our goal.

And there is another matter: some people are saying—'Kenyatta, you and your brothers are now independent, so which side will your independence take you to; will you be pro-West or pro-East, on the side of the devils or the angels?' I therefore declare to you now that the aim of my Government which starts today is not to be pro-Left or pro-Right. We shall pursue the task of nation building, in friendship with the rest of the world. Nobody will ever be allowed to tell us, to tell me: you must be friendly to so-and-so. We shall remain free, and whoever wants friendship with us must be a real friend.

We shall never agree to friendship through any form of bribery. And I want all those nations who are present today—whether from West or from East—to understand our aim. We want to befriend all, and we want aid from everyone. But we do not want assistance from any person or country who will say: Kenyatta, if you want aid, you must agree to this or that. I believe, my brothers, and I tell you now, that it is better to be poor and remain free, than be technically free but still kept on a string. A horse cannot choose: reins can be put on him so he can be led around as his owner desires. We will not be prepared to accept any aid that will tie us like a horse by its reins.

Now my words to the people of Kenya: many people may think that, now there is Uhuru, now I can see the sun of Freedom shining, richness will pour down like manna from Heaven. I tell you there will be nothing from Heaven. We must all work hard, with our hands, to save ourselves from poverty, ignorance and disease.

We ourselves can save us, but nobody else. When the Children of Israel were crying, saying: 'God, why did you bring us to this wilderness, where there is no water or sustenance', God said He would bring them something called manna. This cannot happen again. He said He had closed the door, and anyone who wanted manna had to work for it. These are not the words of Kenyatta. God Himself told the human race. He said He had closed the door with a lock, and had thrown the key into the ocean; that the door would never open again and there would be no more manna in the world.

Therefore, my brothers, we have got to work hard and be faithful, to make our Independence mean all that we want and hope. If we do nothing but sleep, there will be many difficulties. All types of work must be done.

Many people in the world have despised us. I remember one time when I was travelling in Europe, a man told me: 'Kenyatta, the people in your country are very lazy'. When I asked him why, he quoted a story that, since our country was very hot, all we did was sleep under a mango or coconut tree, praying to God that a fruit would fall down while we slept, and then—when it did— waking up to eat it.

From today onwards, I want our Uhuru to mean: 'Uhuru na Kazi . . . Freedom and Work'. This will help us greatly.

Another point, my brothers, is this: do not think that, because there is no longer a Colonial Government, there will no longer be need to respect the country's laws. The laws of the country will remain; the Police and prisons will remain. Do not think that, because the other day I freed about 8,000 people from prison, that all prison doors will be closed and no more people will be sent in. This is not so. Anyone who breaks the laws of the country will be dealt with firmly.

An African Government wants faithfulness. It wants the laws to be obeyed. This is what Government is for, and what it should be. I do not want to burden you. But I do want those who will help me in building our nation, and making it a worthwhile place to live in, to be faithful. Those present who are prepared to help me in this vital task should raise their hands . . . . I thank you all.

I thank you as well for electing me to lead you into a new phase in the progress of our country. In the past, we used to blame the Europeans for everything that went wrong. When things went wrong, we used to say Europeans are bad, they are sucking our blood. When we lacked education, we said the Europeans were only educating their children, and the Asians were only educating their children, so when will ours be educated?

Now the Government is ours. Maybe you will now be blaming Kenyatta, saying: Kenyatta, we elected you, but where is this or that? But you must know that Kenyatta alone cannot give you everything. All things we must do together. You and I must work together to develop our country, to get education for our children, to have doctors, to build roads, to improve or provide all day-to-day essentials. This should be our work, in the spirit that I am going to ask you to echo, to shout aloud, to shatter the foundations of the past with the strength of our new purpose . . . HARAMBEE! . . . HARAMBEE!

A ND then, on the following day at the State Opening of Parliament, Jomo Kenyatta delivered the Address of Thanks:

Mr. Speaker: on behalf of the National Assembly gathered in Parliament, I beg to offer to Her Majesty the Queen this Address of Thanks, for the Gracious Speech which marks the opening of the first Session of Kenya's first independent Parliament.

First, I know that I speak for every Honourable Member of this House, when I express the unbounded pleasure which it gives to each one of us to have His Royal Highness Prince Philip, the Duke of Edinburgh, present here today as Her Majesty's representative.

Mr. Speaker, the aims of the Kenya Government, which have been outlined in the Gracious Speech, are noble objectives; for their achievement, the Government will look to this Parliament and the people of Kenya for guidance and inspiration.

Our Government represents the simple but deep feelings and desires of all our peoples for a better and higher standard of living. We are aware of their great expectations and hopes, and we are resolved not to disappoint them. Our motto of 'harambee' was conceived in the realization of the challenge of nation building that now lies ahead of us. It was conceived in the knowledge that, to meet this challenge, the Government and people of Kenya must pull together. We know that only out of our own efforts and toil can we build a new and better Kenya. This, then, is our resolution.

We may be a very young nation. But we derive great strength from our unity, from our sense of national purpose, and from the determination of our people. As an independent nation, let us face the future with confidence in our ability to build a new Kenya, and to contribute towards the preservation of world peace.

Mr. Speaker, may it please Her Most Gracious Majesty to accept the sincere thanks of this House for the Gracious Speech with which the first Session of our independent Parliament has been opened.

THERE were so many ceremonies and functions, addresses and replies, during the exhaustive and colourful progress of this Uhuru Week. The Prime Minister's pride in all the components of the new Kenya was apparent at all times. One example follows, when—together with His Royal Highness, Prince Philip—he received the Freedom of the City of Nairobi:

In my lifetime, I have seen this fair City of Nairobi grow from the plain—to which the Mayor so eloquently referred—to the fine metropolis of today. I would like to take this opportunity to pay tribute to all those who, down the years, have contributed to Nairobi's great development.

I believe that vigorous and progressive Local Authorities, of which this City Council is such a splendid example, are of vital importance to our whole democratic system of Government, because it is in local government that men and women can most directly exercise the art of self-government. For this reason, my Government attaches the highest importance to the development of local government.

As we stand on the threshold of Independence, I derive great inspiration and encouragement from the growth and progress of our capital City. Let Nairobi be an example to all of us. Let us resolve that, when sixty years hence the people of Kenya look back to this time of Independence, they will be as proud of the growth and progress made by an independent Kenya as we are proud of Nairobi today.

AND later, when all the honoured guests had departed and the bunting was all down, right throughout the stretch of this contemporary period, Mzee Kenyatta lost no opportunity of expressing his own pride in the very sense of freedom, and of reminding the people of the things that freedom means. Here are brief extracts from speeches in Mombasa (February, 1964); Nairobi (two speeches) (June, 1964); Chuka (August, 1964); Embu (August, 1964); and Githunguri (September, 1964). At the end is a quotation from a parliamentary speech in July, 1963:

I am happy also because when we were here last time, we were still fighting for our independence. My joy is that never again must we say that we want our freedom.

*

In the political sphere, we say that liberty is not the mere absence of restraint. Freedom also means the ability to fulfil the meaningful will of the people, and to enjoy a certain area of personal freedom.

*   *   *

You should help the people of this country to live in peace. You should be proud of your freedom. Many of our people died for this freedom, and nobody has the right to meddle with it . . . . Even though we were persecuted, we should not seek revenge. If people were unjust in their day, there is no reason why we should commit injustices. If we did, we should be like them. We must forget all past maltreatment, so that we may build the future of our country.

*   *   *

My joy is your joy, because we are meeting here as free people . . . . Now that we have an African Government, we must appreciate the meaning of freedom. We must obey Government rules, because ours is not a Government of one individual but a Government of all the people.

*   *   *

Many of our people died for freedom . . . . In those days, people thought all who were fighting for freedom were fighting in vain. But yesterday's dream is today's reality: we now have our Uhuru. We will guard Uhuru with all our might.

*   *   *

Had we not fought gallantly for our Uhuru, we would never have sat in an atmosphere of freedom under this tree . . . . There was a section of the Europeans who used to say Kenyatta was bad. But Kenyatta's answer is this: he would rather be in trouble under foreign rule than in peace under imperialist rule.

*   *   *

Uhuru is not for one Party, one community or one group. It is for all people of Kenya to enjoy and breathe the air of freedom, after so many years under the yoke of imperialism and colonialism.

ON May the 28th, 1964, speaking in Nairobi, the Prime Minister made a significant statement on the financial and other complexities of Kenya's Constitution. He announced at that time an extension of the transitional period provided:

Apart from the fact that the first months after Independence are a period of transition, the Kenya Constitution provides for one year of transition, both in the transfer of responsibilities to Regions, and in the financial arrangements underlying both Central and Regional revenues and budgets.

It was also conceded at the time of Independence that Kenya had acquired one of the most complicated Constitutions ever given to a newly-independent State.

My Government has therefore been watching very closely the working of the Constitution, as well as all the developments associated with this transitional period. In this regard, it is proposed to complete the general review of the Constitution later this year. Under this present Constitution, we are experiencing difficulties and problems which must by now be obvious to all.

In view of all the changing circumstances of the present time, and in particular of the review now being made of Kenya's Constitution, the Government has felt it necessary in the national interest to extend the period of transition in respect of the financing of Regional services for a further six months: namely, from July the 1st, to December the 31st.

The consequences of this decision are that the Government financial arrangements now obtaining will continue until the end of this year, and the Government will budget for the services of the nation as a whole, as it has done since Independence. In addition, the Government will exercise supervision over all Public Service establishments. The Minister for Local Government will also be responsible for assisting and supervising the functioning of Local Government Authorities, including their budgets.

I and my Government have taken this decision because of the vital need to protect the public revenues, and to preserve continuity of Government over this period of transition.

THEN on August the 13th, 1964, Mzee Jomo Kenyatta made it clear that Kenya would henceforth work towards a one-Party State. In a lengthy outline of this decision, he reaffirmed that the Africanism needed to meet local needs must be substituted for systems advocated both by West and East, and that national solidarity was an essential factor in Kenya's constitutional development:

On my return from the recent London and Cairo Conferences, I said that from now on we will work towards a one-Party State. Events have shown not only that a one-Party system was inevitable, but also that it was the most prudent method of attaining those aims and objects which our people hold dear.

Our aim in Kenya is to cultivate a social and political order which is consistent with our needs and our conditions. We will borrow what is relevant, and compatible with our aspirations, from any country of the East or West.

Africanism—which continues to gain momentum—will become a powerful instrument for elevating our Continent and accelerating development. In my early days in the political field, I dedicated my book to Africanism, by saying: 'the dead, the living and the unborn will unite to rebuild the destroyed shrines'.

We reject a blueprint of the Western model of a two-Party system of Government, because we do not subscribe to the notion of the Government and the governed being in opposition to one another, one clamouring for duties and the other crying for rights.

Nor are we prepared to justify our predilection for a one-Party system of Government by using the fragile argument that Parties are the expression of social classes, and that therefore there must be only one Party. The theory of class struggle has no relevance to our particular situation here. In a one-Party State such as we envisage, we hold that politics is a potent instrument: it is through our political institutions that we influence economic trends, and not the other way round.

In 1960, after the Constitutional Conference in London, all the Members of Parliament recognized the need for—and reaffirmed their faith in—unity and solidarity, in keeping with the traditional

African way of life. The vanguard of the nationalist struggle for Uhuru was launched. It was only after KANU was formed that several dissidents formed a splinter group, which was later called KADU. It cannot be imagined that these conceited, grasshopper politicians formed their new group because of their belief in majority rule, democracy and the rule of law.

My Government is pledged to uphold the traditional freedoms—of association, speech and assembly—and respect for the rule of law and human dignity. In case of genuine complaints, citizens have recourse to independent Courts of law. In addition, as provided in the Constitution, machinery already exists for a change of Government through free elections at the due time.

It is my considered opinion that the greatest innovation in the political institutions of the world is not the authoritarian regime; dictatorships are as old as the hills.

The fascinating innovation in our time is the mass Party, and the mass Party is to be found both in one-Party and two-Party States. It is the nature of the organization of mass political Parties that is the real threat to the rule of law and democracy. Consequently, there are two-Party States which are tyrannical and dictatorial, and one-Party States which can be said to be democratic and liberal. In other words, all two-Party States are not necessarily democratic, and all one-Party States are not necessarily authoritarian.

Furthermore, those who talk about democracy and individual freedoms must think critically about the position of democracy, in the light of scientific and technological advancement, and especially in the light of the advent of mass media in communications and propaganda.

At this stage, we have no choice to make. Through the historical process which has taken place since the last century, we find ourselves with myriad relevant grounds and conditions for a one-Party State. It is inevitable. In our particular situation, practice will have to precede theory. But should relevant grounds for a multi-Party State evolve in the future, it is not the intention of my Government to block such a trend through prohibitive legislation.

DURING this same month, the Prime Minister referred to the matter again, during speeches at Meru and Githunguri:

KANU has said that Kenya will follow the policy of a one-

Party system, and that we shall work towards this. The trend towards a one-Party system is seen in Tanganyika, Ghana, and many other African nations.

*   *   *

KANU feels that we cannot afford opposition for the sake of opposition. KANU wants a one-Party system in Kenya.

IN the National Assembly on August the 14th, 1964, the Prime Minister announced to the House and to the nation that Kenya would become a Republic on the first anniversary of her Independence. He also gave the first public indication of the form and structure of the new Republican Constitution, to carry Kenya forward into a new status within the Commonwealth of nations. The publication of this book is to mark Republic Day:

During the Election campaign last year, KANU told the country that we would seek to establish in Kenya an independent Republic. It was the wish of the voters that we should have a Republic on the day of Independence, but unfortunately this was not possible due to the length of time taken to finalize the Independence Constitution.

Another important issue on which KANU campaigned was the original nature of the Constitution itself. The majority of voters agree this was too rigid, expensive and unworkable. Since the Election, we have had a chance to note its weakness.

Members will also recall that, during a Debate in June, the Government assured the House of its intention to introduce a Republican Constitution soon. At the same time, in regard to finances of Regions, we informed the country that we were working on certain reforms, and promised to bring these to Parliament when they were ready.

The Government has now decided to introduce a Republican Constitution for Kenya on the first anniversary of our Independence, that is December the 12th this year. With regard to the form of Republican Government to be established under the new Constitution, the Government has carefully considered the various alternative forms, and has decided that the structure must be the one which suited Kenya: it should embody the fact of national leadership as seen in the eyes of the people, the concept of collective Ministerial responsibility, and also guarantee the supremacy of Parliament.

The outline of this proposed Constitution will be: (a) there will be a President who will be the Head of State with executive

Cabinet responsibility to Parliament; (b) the President will be the leader of the majority Party in Parliament, who will appoint his own Cabinet from among the Members of Parliament; (c) the President's full term of office will be related to the life of the Parliament.

It is the intention to maintain Regional Assemblies and Local Government Authorities. However, we propose that the Regional Governments should be controlled on the following lines: (a) Regional Assemblies to have no exclusive executive authority or legislative competence in any matter which should be planned and directed on a national scale: education, agriculture, health, economic and social development, the utilization of land; (b) Local Government Authorities will be controlled directly by the Central Government; (c) the Public Service to be centralized in respect of such matters as appointments, transfers, discipline, postings and promotion. There will no longer be Regional establishments; (d) the Police Force and responsibility for law and order to be a Central Government matter; (e) the Central Government to determine what taxes the Local Government Authorities should levy and what services they should provide. The Government will make up by grants any deficits in Local Government finance.

All land vested in the Regions will be re-vested in the Government without compensation. Trust land will remain vested in the County Councils, but the Government will be empowered to acquire Trust land for national purposes without payment of compensation. The Government will have full control over the utilization of land, and the exploitation of minerals, and benefits of rises in the value of public land will accrue to the Government.

The Government does not intend to make any changes in respect of the fundamental rights provided in the present Constitution, or in respect of citizenship.

We consider it essential for the Public Service Commission to remain executive. This will also take over the functions of the Police Service Commission, and the latter will be abolished.

The Republic of Kenya will continue to be a member of the Commonwealth of Nations.

Details of the new Constitution will be laid before the House and explained by the Minister for Constitutional Affairs. We must in the meantime guard against misrepresentation or deliberate efforts to mislead the country. This move is for a better Kenya.

3

Federation—The Road Ahead

DURING this whole critical period of nearly eighteen months, the Prime Minister—in consultation with the Heads of Government in Tanganyika and Uganda, and assisted by senior colleagues in the Kenya Cabinet—devoted much time and thought to the effective prospect of creating an East African Federation. In his first major parliamentary speech as Prime Minister, on July the 2nd, 1963, Mzee Kenyatta said this:

The first task of my Cabinet, when sworn in on June the 1st, was to send a three-man mission to meet Tanganyika leaders at Arusha. Since then, we have worked together with the leaders of Tanganyika and Uganda, in preparation for an East African Federation within 1963 .... Mr. Sandys assured the Kenya Ministers in London that the British Government, which has long believed in the idea of an East African Federation, supports fully the initiative taken by the East African Governments, and will do all it can to facilitate the early implementation of this aim.

SHORTLY afterwards, he referred to the matter again, stressing both the local importance and the wider perspective of a Federation of East African States. This was on July the 31st, 1963, when the Prime Minister opened a new office of the United Nations Technical Assistance Board in Nairobi:

This matter of the Federation is particularly important to us here in East Africa. We do not want to be separated from our brethren by artificial frontiers, created at the time of Colonialism. We want to work together with them for a better future for all our people. We want to move towards that unity of the East African people in good order, and with our administrative machinery geared to the great task ahead.

In achieving East African unity, we shall be contributing towards a greater unity of the world, through a greater unity of Africa. I will not hide from you that we hope an East African Federation will be one of the cornerstones of African unity, as an indispensable element in building a united world.

A S the New Year dawned, Jomo Kenyatta found himself with early opportunity to pay tribute to one of the major East African Common Services.
Many such services had been functioning for many years—on an East African
basis—especially in all fields of transport and communications. He referred to
'a great moment in the history of East Africa', during a Post Office ceremony
in Nairobi on January the 15th, 1964:

The opening of this new Headquarters . . . (of the East African
Posts and Telecommunications Administration) . . . is a task which
gives me great pleasure. This is an important addition to the good
buildings already erected in East Africa, and although situated
here in Nairobi, it is to be used for the benefit of the general public
of East Africa as a whole.

The Post Office has been an East African service for a long
time. Amalgamation of the individual services in the East African
territories took place in 1933, and the Post Office can therefore
claim to be the oldest member of the Common Services. Its history
can be described as one of service and progress. Since 1948, it has
operated as an entirely self-contained organization, earning its own
revenue and financing its own development. At that time, it took
over from Governments assets valued at £750,000. Today its
assets exceed £23½ million. That is the measure of its development
in fifteen years.

The concept of national frontiers means little to the Post Office.
Through true international co-operation, it is as easy—and sometimes easier—to send a letter to the other side of the world as it is
to a neighbouring town. By providing cheap and speedy means
of communication between peoples of different countries, the
Post Office makes a significant contribution to the improvement
of international understanding and human relationships.

This new Headquarters comes into operation at a great moment
in the history of East Africa. In paying tribute to those responsible
for the wise management and efficient operation of Post Office
services in the past, I wish to express the Authority's confidence
in those men—Africans and their colleagues of other races—who
are taking over responsibility for directing the services in the new
independent East Africa.

O N May the 11th, 1964, the Prime Minister recorded at his Gatundu home
a radio and television message to the whole country. In one passage, he
made reference to political and economic progress towards an East African
Federation, and the question of timing:

The Kenya Government's position on Federation is based on the recent Conference of Heads of Governments, held in Nairobi about mid-April. At that Conference, it was decided to set a Working Party to pursue the objective of forming the Federation, and a Committee to examine certain trade relationships pertaining to the Common Market. This latter Committee has just reported after rapid and friendly discussions, held in all the three Capitals of East Africa. The main Working Party is meeting soon.

I do not consider it necessary to fix yet any target date. The declaration made in June last year, on the formation of Federation, still stands. But we have learnt that a worthwhile target date could only be fixed after all the facts had been fully exposed and considered. In any event, the whole pace towards Federation must be the subject of governmental decisions working through the legislative bodies.

The three Heads of Government have been working for Federation in a brotherly atmosphere. None has rejected Federation; on the contrary, we are all keen to go ahead. The enthusiasm of all people in East Africa for Federation is clearly understood.

ABOUT a month later—June the 17th, 1964—backbench enthusiasm for Federation had mounted, and an Opposition motion calling for accelerated progress was moved in the National Assembly. Mzee Kenyatta intervened in this Debate, to make a major statement. In this, he emphasized that Federation of any meaningful and permanent character, incapable of being wrecked by the first unforeseen problem or hazard, could only be founded on complete agreement, following complete examination of all political and economic factors. The work—he said—was going on:

The only question here is that of ignorance of what has been done by the Heads of State on the issue of East African Federation. I think if the Mover had done a little homework to seek information, he would not have brought this Motion before the House, because he is merely asking the Government to accelerate the machinery to achieve Federation. We thus have no arguments, because this is exactly what the three Governments have been doing.

Some people say: 'let us federate today'. Certainly if you like, but remember that anything in any organization, even a small village organization, needs some machinery to effect that organization. A Federation of three territories such as Kenya, Tanganyika and Uganda is not a joke, and needs a lot of work. The people working on relevant Committees have not just been enjoying themselves. Some of them have sat for hours, sleepless, trying to solve this problem of Federation. You cannot compare the Federation of these three territories with the new union between Tanganyika and Zanzibar.

If KADU really want Federation, they would not behave as they have been behaving. If it were not for the introduction of 'majimbo' . . . (Regionalism) . . . by KADU, Federation would have been much easier. In every Region, each President thinks he is a small king in his domain, and when you speak about Federation in terms of a little 'majimbo' federating with another Government, this cannot be done. The time has come when you must be told the truth. It is a bitter pill, but you can swallow it.

I say this is a question of 'majimbo': a question of division. If you want 'majimbo', you cannot have Federation at the same time. We are going to strip 'majimbo' away and have a proper Federation.

Nobody ever opposed Federation. I and my Government have been working for Federation night and day—you do not know how much. But if you want Federation, the 'majimbo' Constitution must be scrapped. KANU is for unity: one nation, one Government, one flag, and one Africa.

The three Heads of Government are in agreement now—as we were in 1963—that we are for Federation, but people forget that Rome was not built in a day. Federation is not a thing that you can achieve through magic; you have to work and prepare. There are economic factors which have to be sorted out, and political factors which have to be resolved. You cannot just say 'federate!' and be able to act at once. To have a proper Federation, you must work out details, which is why we have the various Committees. The Heads of State are meeting next week here in Nairobi, to discuss the report of the Working Committee which met in Kampala a few weeks ago. The Economic Committee is working—right now—to try and sort out differences.

It is not Nyerere, nor Obote, nor Kenyatta, who is against Federation. We are all for it. We do not reveal all our discussions, since the Government is not run like a newspaper office, or through public meetings. We have done many things which we do not tell you about, but sometimes you see the results.

It is true we made a declaration that we were going to federate at the end of 1963, but it was impossible to do so at that time. We as a Government have laid down our plans, but we cannot do all the things we have promised overnight. Even angels could not do this. It is impossible for me to give you the date when Federation will be. All I can tell you is that we are doing what the Motion has asked: we are accelerating the machinery to effect Federation.

4

Horizons of African Unity

DURING his Kenyatta Day address to the nation, the Prime Minister underlined his dedication—over more than 40 years—to what he described as 'pan-African ideals'. As leader of the new Kenya nation, he concerned himself, with greater directness and authority than had hitherto been possible, to furthering the realistic cause of unity in Africa. In May of 1964, he made a notable reflective statement:

For the first time in an independent Kenya, we celebrate on May the 25th, the first anniversary of the OAU. A year ago on this day, thirty-two Heads of African States signed a Charter in Addis Ababa which established the Organization of African Unity.

I also remember that the setting up of OAU was a fulfilment of forty-four years of sustained struggle for the independence of Africa, which started in Paris in 1919 when the Pan-African Movement gained an organized form. I have myself actively participated in this Movement since its inception, but I would like here to recall the names of my colleagues and co-founders of the Pan-African Movement: the late Doctor William E. B. Dubois and the late George Padmore.

Countrymen, I want to remind you that we fought for Independence to free ourselves from foreign rule. Having done so, we must also liberate our minds and souls from foreign ideas and thoughts. In our own country here, Colonial mentality persists. I should like you to be vigilant, and rededicate yourselves today to building a nation deeply rooted in our own thoughts and ideas. This may mean rewriting school textbooks, evolving new architecture, and songs based on African traditional forms and culture.

We must defend our sovereignty and territorial integrity. Colonialism must be eradicated, and genuine international co-operation and friendship promoted. Guided by the Charter of OAU, Africans are resolved to play a prominent role in the affairs of the United Nations. The achievements of OAU during its one year of

life have demonstrated that Africans can settle amicably contro-
versial and difficult issues.

My Government believes strongly in African unity, and will
strive to broaden the basis of this unity in a manner that reflects
realism. We shall uphold the principle of equality of States, negotiate
disputes peacefully, enhance personal liberty and freedom of expression.

THE theme of African unity was constantly in the Prime Minister's mind.
In the presence of a delegation from Burundi (January, 1964) he said:

As you know, we want African unity, which is not the monopoly
of Kenya, Uganda and Tanganyika. We shall of course extend
unity to Nyasaland, Rhodesia, Ethiopia and Somalia, since we
want Africa to be united.

ON his way back to Nairobi from the 1964 Conference of Commonwealth
Prime Ministers, Mzee Jomo Kenyatta spent some days in Cairo, for
another Conference dealing with the mechanism and effective purpose of African
unity. On July the 30th, 1964, he reported to Parliament:

The House will also be interested to have some account from
me of the Summit Conference of the Organization of African Unity
(OAU), which ended in Cairo last week.

The Assembly approved the establishment of the Commission of
African Jurists, as one of the specialized Commissions of OAU, to
deal with the African judicial system. Another Commission set up
will study the problem of Communications between and among
African States.

As a result of the experience gained during the first year of its
operation, the OAU Summit Conference concluded the Protocol of
Mediation, Conciliation and Arbitration. This was a practical outcome of the determination of member States to have African problems solved in Africa by the Africans themselves. The House will
remember how the boundary disputes between Algeria and Morocco,
and also between Somalia and Ethiopia, have been handled by OAU.

Another significant achievement of the Conference was the
unanimous agreement among the African States to identify the
effort to remove from Africa all Colonial rule and European domination, and to set Africa free for ever. In this respect, the compo-
sition of the Liberation Committee of Nine was approved. Ways
and means of providing more funds to this vital body were also

agreed.

At this Cairo Conference, it was decided to establish a permanent Headquarters for the Organization, and Addis Ababa was chosen. Another step taken to assure the smooth running of the Organization was the appointment of a Secretary-General: Mr. Dialo Telli of Guinea. The Secretary-General will have four Assistants, and you will be glad to know that Kenya was honoured by being asked to fill one of these positions, together with Nigeria, Algeria and Dahomey.

The Kenya delegation played an important part in the Conference, both through formal discussions and constant informal talks. At the opening of the Conference, I was appointed as one of the co-Chairmen. Last but not least, Kenya was unanimously chosen as the venue for the next meeting of the Council of Ministers of the OAU.

THE vision of united Africa, and the role of Africa in refashioning approaches to the problems of mankind, formed the kernel of the Prime Minister's speech at a State Banquet for the Emperor Haile Selassie of Ethiopia. This was on June the 11th, 1964, in the Nairobi City Hall:

Your visit has been the means of cementing the friendship of our two countries, and of the 31 million people who inhabit them. Elsewhere I have mentioned—and it bears repetition—Your Imperial Majesty's enthusiasm for African unity. This aim is shared by me, and by my Government. We must continue, with all the resources which we have, to achieve a united Africa, without which the peoples of this Continent can never gain their rightful place in world affairs.

To achieve this, vision and determination, statesmanship and leadership, are all required. I pray that you will be with us for many years to come, so that Africa may profit from your inspiration. African unity must be encouraged in the spirit of Addis Ababa. Africa must mould herself into a new entity, and as her importance in world affairs increases, she must demonstrate her anxiety to bring about order, stability and understanding in the world; her willingness to accept the rule of law and order at all times; and her wish to live in peace and prosperity without racial or other forms of discrimination.

THIS State visit by His Imperial Majesty was a colourful and popular occasion, with scenes everywhere in Kenya of spontaneous acclaim. During the same State Banquet speech, Jomo Kenyatta struck a personal note:

The people of Kenya have presented you with the gift of a lion and a cheetah. Each of these has its own significance. The lion is a symbol of Royalty and of high courage, and figures prominently in our Coat of Arms. The cheetah runs straight and swiftly to its goal. If I may say so, these qualities are so well blended in your nature and personality that we hope the two animals will serve as token reminders of your visit here.

PERHAPS the most splendid ceremonial of the State visit was recorded on June the 9th, 1964, when the Emperor paid a formal visit to Kenya's Parliament and addressed all Members of the National Assembly. In his reply, the Prime Minister made reference not only to the friendship between Kenya and Ethiopia, but also to the triumph—associated with Ethiopia—of having launched African Unity in its organizational form:

On behalf of myself and of all Members of the National Assembly, I thank Your Majesty . . . (His Imperial Majesty, the Emperor Haile Selassie of Ethiopia) . . . for visiting our Parliament, and for addressing us so graciously.

This has indeed been a great occasion for all of us. As His Excellency the Governor-General has already said, you are the first Head of State to pay a visit here since Kenya became independent. More than this, it is the first time that we have had the opportunity of listening to one of the foremost Elder Statesmen of our time. Let me assure Your Majesty that the people of Kenya rejoice at being able to pay our humble respects to you.

Ethiopia and Kenya have much in common. We have a common boundary; our economies are primarily agricultural and pastoral; we need to develop our industries and strengthen commerce; we need to improve the basic living standards of our peoples. Above all, we must resist our common enemies, not only those who war against us with guns and other weapons, but also the more insidious opponents of disease, ignorance, poverty and illiteracy.

From here, you are also going to see our neighbouring countries of Tanganyika and Uganda. As a result of long association, Kenya, Uganda and Tanganyika have developed common and close ties of friendship. We have a common market; some of our services are operated under the East African Common Services Organization. It is my Government's earnest hope and desire to strengthen our common links in these countries by the formation of a Federation. Your Majesty will recall your initiative in promoting the Pan-African Movement of East and Central Africa. Should the Federation come to reality, it will provide additional manifestation of

Your Majesty's foresight and love of African unity.

The whole world knows that, in Addis Ababa last year, the birth of the Organization of African Unity was a great personal triumph for Your Imperial Majesty. In subscribing to it, this country would like to pay tribute to your vision and statesmanship. Through the Organization, the hopes of creating a strong United Nations Organization have come nearer to reality; so have hopes of liberating from racial domination our brothers in South Africa, Rhodesia, Angola and Mozambique.

I hope this visit will be a prelude to many other visits to Kenya by members of your Government and other citizens of Ethiopia, and that I myself and my Ministers, and officials of my Government, will be privileged to visit Addis Ababa and other parts of Ethiopia, so there may be a constant exchange of ideas and experience from which both our countries may mutually benefit. It is with great satisfaction that we have noted Your Majesty's personal effort in starting to build a highway to make road communication easier between our two Capitals.

I am happy to be able to report that, at long last, agreement has been reached on the delineation of the frontier between Ethiopia and Kenya. This has been the result of many years of patient survey.

We have also agreed that every effort must be made to control border raiding, which has been a source of constant anxiety to me and my people. Many innocent lives have been lost. The Governments both of Ethiopia and Kenya will do everything in their power to put an end to these frontier incidents, and to persuade the inhabitants of the frontier areas to live in peace with their neighbours.

From the time I first met Your Imperial Majesty about thirty years ago, we have remained good friends. During this time, my esteem and affection for Your Majesty have continued to grow unceasingly. Ethiopia fought and won her freedom, and then joined the world to free mankind from Fascism. We in Kenya have also struggled, and have won our independence. I must assure Your Majesty that it is a great joy for the people of Kenya, and myself personally, to be able to welcome you to this Parliament in your rightful capacity as Emperor of one of the oldest free nations of the world.

Long live brotherhood between Ethiopia and Kenya. Long live African Unity.

BUT against all the background of constructive and positive work, and of high hopes for the creation and impact of unity in Africa, were sombre difficulties within Kenya herself. These arose through a claim, by the neighbouring Republic of Somalia, to large areas of territory in the north-eastern quadrant of Kenya. This claim became supported by increasing agitation and unrest. Within the period covered by this contemporary narrative, the first main event was a meeting—between delegations from Kenya and Somalia—held in Rome. Due to other commitments, Mzee Kenyatta was unable to attend, and then on September the 5th, 1963, speaking in Nairobi, he said this:

The statement reported to have been made a few days ago by my friend the Prime Minister of Somalia, that my inability to attend the Rome Conference was due to a 'diplomatic illness', is wholly incorrect.

I very much regretted that I could not fulfil my intention to lead the group of Kenya Ministers at the Rome Conference. Now, I need only say that the proposals made by them at Rome still stand.

My colleagues and I will be glad to resume discussions with representatives of the Somalia Government at an early date, concerning relations between Kenya and Somalia, if the Somalia Government is ready to meet us in the same spirit of African brotherhood and neighbourliness which animates us.

The detailed proposals made by the Kenya Government in Rome were as follows:

(a) Primary consideration will be given to the welfare of the inhabitants of the North Eastern Region;

(b) Agreement shall be sought by peaceful and lawful means, and all concerned will co-operate to reduce tension in the area;

(c) Her Majesty's Government will take no unilateral decision involving a change in the frontiers of Kenya before Independence;

(d) With these points in mind, then: (i) the Kenya Government recognizes the interest of Somalia in the future of any people of Somali origin residing in Kenya; (ii) the Somalia Government and the Kenya Government, taking into account previous contacts, will resume discussions at an early date to be agreed; (iii) if these discussions do not result in agreement, the Kenya Government accepts that the Somalia Government will be free—after Kenya's independence—to bring the matter to the notice of African States within the spirit of the Addis Ababa resolutions; (iv) the Government of Kenya, in consultation with Her Majesty's Government, is actively considering what further steps should be taken to provide for the particular needs of the inhabitants of the area.

A T the Airport a few days later—September the 21st—he made further reference to Rome, before leaving for the final Constitutional Conference in London:

The Rome talks have placed the issue of the North Eastern Region rightly where it belongs. It is not a subject for discussion at the London talks, but is a matter for the Kenya Government. Settlement of this issue will only be possible in an African context.

O N February the 26th, 1964, the Prime Minister made a major parliamentary speech on this issue. By then, a State of Emergency had been declared in the North Eastern Region of Kenya. The Prime Minister gave the House details of past and pending attacks by armed gangs. He spoke of propaganda by Mogadishu Radio, and the 'policy of territorial expansion' practised by the Government of Somalia. Then—Mzee declared—'you cannot settle problems by shooting', and so, mindful of obligations and with faith in its purpose, Kenya had raised the whole matter with the Organization of African Unity:

I am moving a resolution to extend a State of Emergency in the North Eastern Region, in accordance with a constitutional provision designed to give the National Assembly an opportunity to review any Emergency situation.

Prior to the declaration of a State of Emergency on December the 25th last, some 34 incidents occurred in the North Eastern Region. Bandits attacked Police stations, Police posts and military units, and the series of attacks commenced with the abdication of the President of the Northern Frontier Independence Party in November. On the whole, the attacks—mainly at night—were not very successful. But they were of nuisance value, and were hampering the plans of the Kenya Government to apply the country's Constitution in this Region. Furthermore, the population of the area appeared reluctant to assist the security forces in detection of the gangs.

The Emergency Order brought into being a prohibited area five miles in width along the border of Kenya and Somalia. It also gave security forces powers of detention in respect of persons found in the prohibited area. Regulations make it an offence for anyone in the North Eastern Region to assist the shifta . . . (bandits) . . . and detention powers apply to such offenders.

Early in January, gang attacks stopped in the border area, but several gangs penetrated deep into the North Eastern Region, where they made well organized and concerted attacks on patrols and camps. The whole pattern changed, as civilians in the Region were attacked, presumably to instil fear into the local population to promote a policy of non-co-operation with the Kenya Government and security forces. This appears to have been successful in some areas, where attacks and ambushes by shifta achieved some success against security forces. However, the killing of civilians had angered some sections of the population, and political leaders and Chiefs in the Region became more readily agreeable to co-operate with the Kenya Government.

It is a significant fact that among us today are Elected Members from the Region. It is a sure demonstration of the faith placed upon the Government by the people, and a step forward in integration of the Region into the economic and political life of Kenya.

When the plans for election were announced, Mogadishu Radio increased its campaign of hate against me and against the Government of Kenya. Coinciding with this propaganda, shifta gangs infiltrated deep into Kenya, and even into parts of the Eastern and Coast Regions. During this month, it has become evident that the gangs had obtained a plentiful supply of arms, ammunition and grenades. They have launched a series of well organized and concerted attacks against the Kenya Army, the Kenya Police, and Government Officers.

The security forces have been hampered in their operations by the continuance of the short rains. During the first part of January, all supplies of food and ammunition had to be flown into most areas of the North Eastern Region and parts of the Eastern Region. The continued rain resulted in an abundance of water and thick bush. This enabled the shifta gangs to move and conceal themselves at will, with little fear of detection once an engagement had been broken off.

The State of Emergency has assisted the security forces by: (a) restricting movements across the border into Somalia via the introduction of a prohibited zone; (b) detention of persons believed to be assisting the gangs; (c) making it an offence for any person in the region to assist the shifta; (d) making all offences under the Regulations cognizable to the Police.

Indications are that attacks by the gangs will become more determined and more frequent in the next few weeks. It is essential that the State of Emergency shall continue to apply in all parts of the North Eastern Region, if the activities of the security forces are to be effective in eliminating the gangs.

There is no doubt at all that the Somalia Government's policy of territorial expansion has led to the killing of peaceful Kenya citizens, straining our relations with that Government. Mindful of this country's obligations in the maintenance of peace and security, and in accordance with their own declaration, the Kenya Government raised the matter in an emergency Council of Ministers meeting of OAU held in Dar es Salaam two weeks ago. The Council decided to include the matter on the Agenda of its meeting now under way in Lagos.

It is my hope that, from what is said there, the Somalia Government will be able to see the light and stop activities likely to endanger peace in eastern parts of Africa.

To the people who live in the North Eastern Region, I have this to say: we know that many of you are herdsmen during the day and shifta at night. Others conceal shifta and refuse to give information about their movements. The voice of Somalia Radio talks of murder and hate. It is you who suffer most by the hands of terrorists. Government can apply measures which could hurt both the innocent and the guilty, but the Government has so far refrained from applying such measures in the hope that co-operation will be forthcoming. There are signs that this co-operation is being given, and—insofar as I am assured of a fair response to my appeal—I propose to maintain the present policy. But I will not hesitate to increase the severity of penalties if the situation deteriorates.

We are faced with a very grave situation. Some people in the House would applaud loudly if I said I would issue orders for the Army to shoot on sight. But this I will not do, because we are human beings, and sometimes—whether we are angry or not—we must act as human beings. This is not the way to settle problems: you cannot settle problems by shooting. I consider the Somalis in the North Eastern Region as our brothers. You have to negotiate with your brothers, you have to talk to them. We have to conduct negotiations, and we have to fight the shifta. The Government is fully prepared to fight the shifta and wage war against them, but we are not going to wage war against the people of the North Eastern Region.

Some Members may think we are weak, and wonder why we have not attacked the Somalia Government. Unlike the case of Ethiopia—where Somalis in force crossed the border and were given the lesson they deserved—they have not dared to come anywhere near our border. They have employed our own Somalis in the North Eastern Region, and it is not easy to sort out in the population who is shifta and who is not. But we are taking all necessary steps.

I do not think the time has come to fight Somalia. We can protest, but the Somalis have not yet crossed our border. If we want peace, agree with me, let us stand on our border and say: 'We are guarding our border; shifta or no shifta, Somalia or no Somalia, we will not let anyone cross our boundary'.

We have every confidence in the fighting forces, our security forces, in northern Kenya. Together with the Administration, they are working hard under very difficult conditions.

WHEN he inaugurated the Kenya Air Force on June the 1st, 1964, the first anniversary of Internal Self-government, the Prime Minister made this comment:

There are many forces which are sometimes subtle, but at times openly very aggressive—such as those in the North Eastern Region —which seek to destroy what we are building . . . . I must tell you, and firmly tell you, that our Government is vigilant. By the sacrifice of numerous nationalists, our freedom was won. It is now your duty to maintain and safeguard, never to lose this hard-won freedom.

A week later (June the 9th), in the course of his reply in the National Assembly to the Address by the Emperor Haile Selassie, Mzee Kenyatta again denounced territorial expansion, and spoke of mutual co-operation between African States:

Our problems are those of many other of the developing countries of Africa. They can only be solved by hard and patient toil, by the utilization of all available resources, and by mutual co-operation between the countries of Africa and the world. With these objects in view, our two countries have denounced those possessed with unholy ideas of territorial expansion.

I am glad to be able to tell the House that Kenya has completed a defence treaty with Ethiopia, which will provide for mutual assistance should this be necessary. Furthermore, the Ethiopian Government has agreed to make training facilities available to the Kenya armed forces, and it has been agreed that there will be co-operation between our Governments to protect those of our peoples who live on our frontiers.

A GAIN in the House (July the 30th, 1964), the Prime Minister made further mention—in the context of African unity—of the agreement between Kenya and Ethiopia. Kenya's attitude and actions have since then continued to be in accord with the Charter of the OAU:

At the Foreign Ministers' Conference which preceded the Summit Conference of the OAU in Cairo, an item was brought up for discussion by the Somali delegation alleging that there were inherent dangers in concluding Regional Military Agreements. This was successfully voted out of the Agenda by an overwhelming majority: 27 to 3 with one abstention. The item was clearly intended against the military pact between Ethiopia and Kenya, and the vote was taken after the Kenya delegation had made a firm statement justifying the action of the two countries, which was in accord with the Charter of the OAU.

THE influence of Kenya—and especially of the Prime Minister personally —in work to settle outstanding issues in Africa through the inspiration and strength of unity, was illustrated in September, 1964, through Jomo Kenyatta's appointment as Chairman of a special Commission on the Congo. He welcomed Commission members to Nairobi on September the 18th:

It is with sincere satisfaction . . . . (as Chairman of the *ad hoc* Commission on the Congo) . . . . that I stand here to welcome you all . . . .(Secretary-General, and delegates from Cameroun, Ethiopia, Ghana, Guinea, Nigeria, Somalia, Tunisia, United Arab Republic and Upper Volta) . . . to Kenya on the occasion of this historic meeting, called by the Organization of African Unity to attempt to find a solution to the problems of the Congo Leopoldville.

Our task is difficult and delicate. Others have tried to find a settlement of the issues which face us. We shall use their experience, but avoid their pitfalls. Some people have predicted that we are doomed to fail, and to such people I have this to say: if anyone started a race assured of success, there would be no point in starting. Our approach is to try and try again to find a solution in an African context.

The over-riding consideration in our deliberations is the fate of our brothers in the Congo Leopoldville. We want to help them to live in peace and unity, and in harmony with their neighbours.

I believe that victory—to be lasting—must be shared, for rarely in history does one side gain the whole victory. I trust, therefore, that we can achieve our aim if we adopt an attitude of give and take.

The maturity of this Commission will be judged by its force of reason and persuasion. Already, we are inspired by the spirit of co-operation and understanding which was created in Addis Ababa a few weeks ago. Let that spirit once again reign in this Conference Hall.

THEN, at a major news conference in Nairobi on September the 20th, the Prime Minister reported to the world on the hopeful work of this Commission:

What I shall be giving you now is a progress report on the work of the Commission . . . . (the *ad hoc* Commission on the Congo, also known as the Kenyatta Commission) . . . . This work will continue, and the Commission will visit Brazzaville, Congo Leopoldville and Burundi to see things for itself, on the spot.

I will first read to you an official communiqué:

'The OAU Congo *ad hoc* Commission met under the effective Chairmanship of Mr. Jomo Kenyatta at Nairobi on September the 18th, in accordance with the decision previously taken at Addis Ababa.

'Lengthy statements by the Prime Minister of the Democratic Republic of the Congo, and the Foreign Ministers of the Kingdom of Burundi and of the Republic of the Congo (Brazzaville), greatly assisted the accomplishment of the Commission's mandate.

'In an atmosphere of complete frankness and fraternity, an agreement has been reached . . . . (between the Prime Minister and two Foreign Ministers quoted above) . . . . on the following points:

'The representatives of the three Governments have agreed with the Commission to co-operate fully in implementation of Para. 8 of the Addis Ababa resolution;

'The Democratic Republic of the Congo undertakes to facilitate the cessation of hostilities in accordance with Para. 4 of the resolution of the Council of Ministers of OAU;

'The representatives of the three Governments have reiterated the invitation addressed to the Commission to visit their respective countries. They have promised to provide facilities, and particularly to facilitate contacts deemed necessary by the Commission with the leaders of those fighting, in order to encourage national reconciliation within the Democratic Republic of the Congo.

'The following resolution was then moved by the representative of Guinea, and adopted by the Commission:

'The delegation of the Government of the Democratic Republic of the Congo is requested to deposit with the Secretariat a report setting forth concrete proposals relating to the items on the Commission's agenda, namely (a) national reconciliation; (b) normalization of relations between the Democratic Republic of the Congo and its neighbours, the Kingdom of Burundi and the Republic of Congo (Brazzaville);

'The delegations of the Kingdom of Burundi and the Republic of Congo (Brazzaville) are each requested to deposit with the Secretariat a report setting forth in concrete terms the proposals which they submit to the Commission, with a view to achieving normalization of their respective relations with the Democratic Republic of the Congo;

'The Commission has decided to examine the reports, and to discuss them fully with the Governments concerned, before submitting its final report to the Secretariat of the Organization of African Unity.'

(Mzee Kenyatta then continued) ' . . . . I wish to take this opportunity of thanking the Prime Minister of Congo Leopoldville, the Foreign Minister of Congo Brazzaville, and the representative of the Kingdom of Burundi, for their useful contributions and co-operation in assisting the Commission in its work.

'I wish to inform the general public that we will be resuming our meeting in Nairobi to prepare our future activities, and to make arrangements about visiting the three territories. We feel we cannot accomplish our task sitting here in Nairobi. We must visit these countries to see things for ourselves, and be able to discuss things on the spot with the representatives of the three Governments.'

5

The Challenge to Apartheid

DESPITE all the commitments and pressures of nation building in Kenya the Prime Minister at no time relaxed his efforts—in company with other African leaders—to condemn and seek an end to apartheid policies and racial brutalities in South Africa. On July the 30th, 1964, in a report to Parliament he made formal comment:

Another crucial matter which was emphasized by the African leaders . . . (at the Commonwealth Prime Ministers' Conference in London) . . . was that of South Africa. We pointed out that some Commonwealth countries treated South Africa as though she was still a member of the Commonwealth, despite her continued racial policies. We also called for a complete ban on the supply of arms, compliance with the United Nations resolution, and application of economic sanctions.

IN almost every comprehensive speech (as here, at a dinner in Mombasa on February the 22nd, 1964) he touched on this issue:

Kenya has already proved that people of different races can live together in peace. In this respect, we have a lot to teach South Africa regarding co-existence.

IN the middle of 1964, Mzee Kenyatta's warnings to the South African Government—and indeed his strictures to mankind—reached a climax. Following the outcome of the Mandela trial, he used these words, speaking in Nairobi on June the 17th:

The Kenya Government is appalled at the sentences of life imprisonment imposed upon Mr. Nelson Mandela and other nationalists in South Africa. The trial and its outcome were yet one more manifestation of the evil racialist philosophy which grips the minority rulers of South Africa. This ugly racialism means the killing of the innocent, and Police brutality. It means the denial of even the most fundamental rights to those who have a dark skin and are not regarded as citizens and human beings in the land of their birth.

Yet even those who practise the system of apartheid know within their hearts that democracy and freedom are soon coming. The people will not be bought off with Bantustans. They want a democratic South Africa in which black, brown and white will govern and work and play together, not in suspicious separation.

Leaders such as Nelson Mandela may be imprisoned and tortured and restricted, but we know they will not surrender. Their cause is just, and it will prevail. We too have experienced the hand of oppression, and we triumphed. The peoples' leaders in South Africa take heart from the lessons which the history of our Continent can teach about the triumph of democracy over racialism and Colonialism.

They will be sustained also by the knowledge that they have the support of millions of people throughout the African Continent, and indeed throughout the world.

I give a pledge that Kenya will do all that is within its power to bring about the liberation of South Africa. We have already made considerable sacrifices in the implementation of the trade boycott. There may be greater contributions for us to make. I am confident that the people of Kenya will gladly make any sacrifice that may be asked of them for their South African brothers.

So long as racialism rules in lands to the south of us, we cannot ourselves feel fully free.

FOUR days later (June the 21st, 1964), a major protest rally—against South Africa—was held in Nairobi. One of the largest crowds seen for some time was addressed by the Prime Minister, who began his speech in this way:

Our freedom will be useless if our brothers continue to be enslaved in South Africa. We shed our blood in this country, and experienced persecution till we won. In the same way, we shall fight for our colleagues. We stand together with our brothers, and will do everything in our power to liberate them . . . There are Boers who are enjoying themselves in this country. Not one of them has condemned the South African apartheid policy. We shall condemn these people in the same way as we condemn South Africa. If they call themselves citizens of this country, let them decry and malign the policies of the South African régime.

THEREAFTER, developing his theme, Jomo Kenyatta placed the issue of South Africa in the whole context of world stability. He warned that the present South African Government was fomenting such racial bitterness as to risk the spread of violence based simply on race. And then, the Prime Minister threw out a challenge, especially to the Western world, to support the African nations in all non-violent measures, instead of paying lip-service to the African attitude in principle, while continuing commercially to do what seemed expedient:

South Africa, so long as the current undemocratic system prevails there, represents a threat to the peace of the whole Continent, and indeed to the stability of the whole world.

I have said before, and I will say it again, that we shall do everything in our power to bring democracy to South Africa. The people of South Africa have made it clear that they are not going to be fobbed off with Bantustans in place of democracy. They want to build a country where race is not of importance, and where all will have equal rights. We will support them in that desire.

I like to think that—in a small way—we in Kenya and in East Africa are already demonstrating that peoples of different races and tribes can live together in one state of harmony. I hope that we are showing that white racialism need not be replaced by black racialism.

There are still signs in South Africa itself that the Africans are prepared to accept the Europeans as brothers. Many Europeans and Asians, and other non-Africans, are still prepared to work alongside the African leaders. Many of them are suffering for sticking to their principles. Some were tried and sentenced as colleagues of Nelson Mandela.

I pray that Verwoerd and his fellow-racialists will not goad and goad the Africans, to a point where the nationalist movement is driven to oppose the white man as such. I have enough faith in humanity to believe that this will not happen, however much Verwoerd may be promoting this by his actions.

As I have said, it is not only the security of Africa, but the peace of the whole world, which is threatened by the continuance of apartheid. It is vitally important that the system should be ended as quickly as possible. The longer it continues, the more likely does it become that the situation could erupt into a world explosion.

We of Africa, and many countries of Asia, and some elsewhere in the world, have already given support to the people of South Africa, by means of the trade boycott and sanctions and in more direct ways. We have been supported, and have been promised more direct aid, by a number of States outside Africa.

Yet the countries of the West—and Britain and the United States in particular—pay lip-service to our cause, while they go on underpinning the South African economy by their investments, their buying and their sales. And it is critics in those countries who are stupid enough to accuse us of bringing the Cold War to Africa, when we declare our readiness to accept aid in our struggle from other sources. We do not want the South African issue to become part of the Cold War. We want all the nations of the world to help us in our struggle for freedom in South Africa.

By refusing to participate in workable sanctions against South Africa, the countries of the West are creating a situation in which violence becomes the only answer. If, by their neglect to take non-violent measures, there is fighting and bloodshed, where will the countries of the West stand then? Will they be with us or against us?

For more than half a century, the African nationalist movement in South Africa—supported by many individual non-Africans—has based itself upon the principles of non-violence.

In a most moving address during his trial a few weeks ago, Nelson Mandela explained why he and his colleagues were driven to a position where sabotage had to be embarked upon in the struggle for their rights. How much more bitterness will the white racialists who rule South Africa stir up before they are finished? The recent history of Africa shows well enough that violence will only beget violence, but that the forces of freedom and justice will prevail.

A ND the mounting tension in Southern Rhodesia was at no time overlooked. In the parliamentary speech (July, 1964) which followed his London visit, the Prime Minister made these points:

The problems posed by Southern Rhodesia were discussed at length . . . (by the Commonwealth Prime Ministers' Conference in London) . . . The African leaders made it clear that Britain must accept responsibility here. She must do more than intervene in the affairs of Southern Rhodesia.

Three points made right at the start of these discussions were: (a) that continued weakening of African political leaders in Southern Rhodesia would lead to a loss of control over the African masses, and make the solution to Southern Rhodesia more intractable.

Therefore we demanded the immediate release of the African nationalist leaders, such as Nkomo and Sithole, from imprisonment and detention; (b) that Britain must call a Constitutional Conference of all parties to work out a Constitution for majority rule in Southern Rhodesia based on one-man, one-vote; (c) that unilateral declaration of independence by the present European minority Government of Southern Rhodesia would not be acceptable, and firm measures would be taken in such an eventuality.

I was more than gratified at the response in the meeting to the African standpoint in this regard, and recognition by Britain that she has responsibilities to the Commonwealth in this respect.

6

Africa in World Society

DURING the August speech in which he outlined plans for Kenya to become a Republic, the Prime Minister made it clear that the new Republic would continue to be a member of the Commonwealth of nations. Mzee Kenyatta has constantly held that such membership, involving no loss of sovereignty, gave the country an opportunity to join with others in working for inter-racial harmony, economic reform, and world peace. On November the 13th, 1963, speaking in Parliament, he said this:

Agreement was reached during the London Conference that, on attaining Independence, we should seek membership of the Commonwealth.

The Commonwealth is a free association of sovereign independent countries, recognized as separate international entities enjoying equal status. It is not a collection of subject nations. Both Tanganyika and Uganda are members of the Commonwealth. South Africa has already been expelled.

I wish to inform the House that the Commonwealth is an association for the promotion of understanding amongst its peoples, and for world peace. Membership of the Commonwealth does not involve any surrender of sovereignty, nor will it in any way qualify Kenya's Independence. By joining the Commonwealth, Kenya does so freely, and—like all other members—reserves her right to withdraw from the association if it should be held to be in the national interest.

SOME months later—on July the 30th, 1964—shortly after he had returned from London and Cairo, Jomo Kenyatta reported to the National Assembly on his meeting with other Commonwealth leaders:

I am glad to have this opportunity of reporting to the House on the 13th Commonwealth Prime Ministers' Conference held in London from July the 8th to the 15th. Kenya played a major role in all discussions.

Kenya was honoured by being asked to respond to the

Chairman's welcoming message. At this stage of the Conference, I said that unless the Commonwealth was able to resolve the problems of race among its members, it would remain an ineffective force.

In further discussion which followed the first meeting, I made it clear that Kenya follows a policy of non-alignment in world affairs, and that our position in this regard must be accepted. I added that Kenya did not attend the meeting with the intention of planning or plotting with one Cold War bloc or power against another. We were vitally concerned with the establishment of peace and tranquillity in the world, but countries committed to the West should fully accept that Kenya does not have to agree or approve their conduct in the Cold War.

On economic subjects, I said that aid—no matter how freely given—was not the final answer for the developing countries. Steps must be taken to review the danger of economic exploitation or domination. It is necessary to expand trade and markets for products from the developing countries, and to abandon protectionist policies and quota systems as applied by some of the developed countries.

As regards the call for inter-racial harmony in the world, there was a definite commitment for each Commonwealth country to build a society providing for equal opportunities and non-discrimination for all its people. In this respect, I did not hesitate to quote the example of Kenya.

A quorum so representative of people as the Commonwealth can be a great force for good. We in Kenya should feel proud to belong to a group which has recognized the need for racial harmony in the world.

APART from all the principles of Commonwealth status and objective, the Prime Minister has all along been concerned with those practical patterns of philosophy or machinery which members of the Commonwealth could offer or suggest to one another, for local adaptation. In particular, there is the system of parliamentary procedure, which each country has to work out for itself. At a Dinner given by the Commonwealth Parliamentary Association in Nairobi, on July the 26th, 1963, Mzee Kenyatta remarked:

Here in Kenya, the parliamentary system is in everybody's blood, but what is not yet certain is the particular type of parliamentary system that we shall evolve for Kenya. I do not know whether democracy—such as is practised in the United Kingdom—

1—Mzee Kenyatta being sworn in as Kenya's first Prime Minister on Internal Self-government Day.

2—The Prime Minister garlanded by young girls during an early official visit to Nakuru.

3—Jomo Kenyatta addressing an impromptu meeting while on tour in the Western Region.

4—The Prime Minister watching elephant at Kilaguni when on his way back from the Coast.

5—Mzee Jomo Kenyatta holding aloft the Constitutional Instruments in the Stadium on Uhuru Day.

6—The Prime Minister receiving the Freedom of the City of Nairobi from Mayor Rubia.

7—Mzee Kenyatta with the members of his Cabinet and some senior officials following Independence.

8—The Prime Minister at the Academic Ceremony where he was elected an Honorary Fellow.

9—Jomo Kenyatta listening to the Kenya Rifles band playing the revised National Anthem.

10—The Prime Minister on a tour of cattle exhibits at the Elgeyo-Marakwet County Show in Kenya's Rift Valley.

11—Mzee Jomo Kenyatta being decorated by the Emperor Haile Selassie with the Distinguished Order of the Queen of Sheba at State House in Nairobi.

12—The Prime Minister standing outside Parliament Buildings in Nairobi with (left) President Julius Nyerere of Tanganyika and (right) Prime Minister Milton Obote of Uganda.

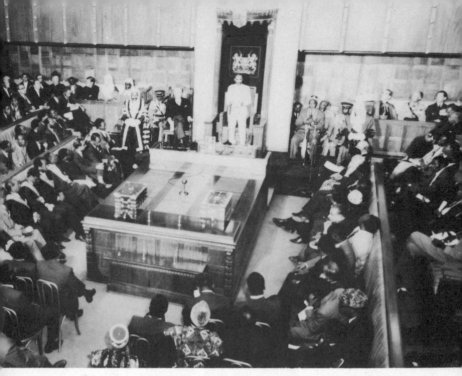

13—Mzee Kenyatta listening to Emperor Haile Selassie during his State Visit to Kenya's Parliament.

14—The Prime Minister and Cabinet Ministers outside Kenyatta National Hospital with Emperor Haile Selassie.

15—Jomo Kenyatta standing with a number of colleagues in the Oil Refinery at Changamwe, Mombasa.

16—Mzee Kenyatta pictured with a group of Masai moran during a visit to Narok, Masailand.

17—The Prime Minister approaching his aircraft to attend the Commonwealth Conference in London.

18—Mzee Jomo Kenyatta inspecting a Kenya Rifles Guard of Honour at Nairobi Airport.

19—The Prime Minister at the opening of a Conference of Speakers and Clerks in Nairobi.

20—Mzee Kenyatta opening the OAU's ad hoc Congo Commission in the Nairobi City Hall.

21—Jomo Kenyatta inspecting a Guard of Honour mounted by the National Youth Service in Nairobi.

22—The Prime Minister laying the foundation stone of the new Githunguri Secondary School in Kenya's Fort Hall District.

will be the best system for this country. But being individualists, we will work out our own system, based on our own traditions and methods, and taking into account our particular mode and way of life.

Our Parliament here in Kenya is not merely for the making of laws. It is a forum, where people drawn from all sections may air their grievances and find ways of settling them. People must have a place where they can meet and exchange their views, where they can discuss their problems. Parliament is a sort of safety-valve, and if it did not exist, the grievances which people had would burst out in some undesirable form.

Our Parliament is a place for discussion. In the House, we are often violent towards one another, but when we come out we meet in a friendly spirit, and the fiercest rivals can be seen cracking jokes with one another. I am proud of this Parliament. And although I may get angry in the Chamber, I never carry such a feeling outside.

Everyone in this country must do what he can to make this Parliament of ours a place for fostering friendship and for solving problems. It must be a place where we can discuss our differences and create harmony between all: between every citizen and every Member. From Parliament, we must spread the spirit to our people, to work together to build up a new Kenya.

MUCH later, he pursued this same theme: the welding of the African personality into the essential duty and dignity attached to parliamentary functions. On this occasion (August the 12th, 1964) the Prime Minister was welcoming to Nairobi a Conference of Speakers and Clerks:

On behalf of my Government and people, it gives me great pleasure to welcome Speakers and Clerks of Parliaments from Uganda, Northern Rhodesia, Southern Rhodesia, Malawi, the East African Central Legislative Assembly, and the Clerk of the House of Commons.

I understand that this is a unique Conference, and that it is perhaps the first of its kind in the Commonwealth. I am thus particularly pleased that it is taking place in Kenya.

The importance of Speakers of Parliaments—representing countries which have just gained or are about to gain Independence —being able to meet and exchange ideas, and to share their experiences, cannot be exaggerated.

Parliamentary procedures in the Commonwealth have been

modelled on those of the British Parliament, but at the same time the independent countries are looking for procedures which they can understand, and which reflect their new image.

I hope that as a result of a Conference such as this, a study will be made of parliamentary procedures which—though modelled on those of the Mother of Parliaments—will express the African personality.

In young countries we must maintain high respect and dignity, without which our Parliaments will be unable to fulfil efficiently their functions as law-making bodies.

NOT merely out of courtesy, but also from deep satisfaction, the Prime Minister was scrupulous in acknowledging—himself—any event, tangible or symbolic, marking closer ties between Kenya and Commonwealth countries. As an instance (September, 1964):

I have received with pleasure and satisfaction the report of the Minister for Justice and Constitutional Affairs, Mr. Mboya, about his visit to Australia. I want to express my appreciation to the Australian Government for their hospitality to the Minister and his wife, and for the promise of technical educational aid. Details of this aid will be announced shortly.

BUT on May the 25th, 1964, in a message on Commonwealth Day, Mzee Kenyatta reminded fellow members of this worldwide union that there were still frustrations in Africa, and not yet was there a universal fabric of free and equal association, on which alone the Commonwealth could be maintained:

Our participation in observing Commonwealth Day is a mark of the close co-operation which exists, within the Commonwealth countries which compose this association of nations which are equal in status. At times, relationships between member States have been strained, but the Commonwealth has survived as a source of power in fighting ignorance, disease and poverty.

However, I should like to take this opportunity to remember our African brethren still in bondage. I refer to Africans in South Africa, Southern Rhodesia, and Portuguese Colonies. Our stand in freeing our brethren cannot be compromised, and Kenya will take every opportunity provided by the Commonwealth meeting in July to urge the acceptance of our view in this matter. It is only after our brethren are free that we can all celebrate Commonwealth Day together without misgivings.

BEYOND the Commonwealth: the world. Kenya became a full member of the United Nations on attaining Independence, and the Prime Minister has associated his country's beliefs and activities with the ideal concept of a 'free and united world'. On July the 31st, 1963, at a United Nations ceremony in Nairobi, he made these comments:

I cannot open the Office of the United Nations Technical Assistance Board ... (and Special Fund) ... without telling you how much we, the Government of this country, appreciate the role of the United Nations in Africa. We appreciate particularly what you—the people administering Technical Assistance and the Special Fund—have done, are doing, and I hope will continue to do, for Kenya and for East Africa as a whole.

We are glad that there are, at this moment in East Africa, working with us and for the good of our people, 156 specialists of a number of different nationalities, engaged under various programmes sponsored by the United Nations and its Specialized Agencies. Of this total, 32 are in Kenya. I can tell you they are welcomed and appreciated, not only by the Departments and Institutions that they are working with, but also by the people.

Many more are due to arrive over the next few months, as more projects get under way and others are expanded. We have asked for all these men and women to come and help us in our economy, our agriculture, on irrigation work, in co-operative societies, in education, in health services, and all the other things that our people need.

Nor do we forget that your assistance is not limited to the provision of experts. The United Nations and its Specialized Agencies provide fellowships, equipment, courses, and advisory services.

I want you particularly to understand that what we are trying to achieve here is a step towards that ideal of a free and united world which the United Nations is striving to bring about.

AND then, on United Nations Day in October, 1964, in an address to a commemorative parade in the centre of Nairobi, Mzee Jomo Kenyatta used these words:

It is with great pleasure—shared by the Government and people of Kenya—that I take part today in this ceremony, marking the 19th anniversary of the founding of the United Nations.

This is a well-chosen day for celebration in our Continent, since our good wishes go out to the newly-independent Republic of Zambia, now able to make a full and sovereign contribution to world affairs.

A principal motive for the foundation of the United Nations, at the end of the Second World War, was to save future generations of mankind from the sufferings and wastage of global conflict. But motive without vision is seldom enough. The effectiveness of this world forum was found in its Charter. Its provisions and purposes had the simplicity of greatness: to enshrine the dignity of man; to codify and preserve human rights; to recognize the equality and respect the integrity of member nations; to champion justice under international law; to instil respect for freely-entered obligations; and to use world resources in science and technology to combat poverty, illiteracy, sickness and malnutrition.

The world today, although beset by problems and suspicions, knows more stability than would have been possible without United Nations efforts. Its achievements have therefore been critical. And the success of this world body has reflected the sum total of selfless goodwill and contribution from all member States.

Among the forty-six countries represented at the foundation meeting, at San Francisco in 1945, only two—Ethiopia and Liberia—were African States. Since then, many more African countries have achieved their independence, releasing their talents and energies and philosophies for the service of the family of nations. Today, thirty-four member States from Africa have seats at the United Nations, and more will follow shortly.

My Ministers and I have said many times that Kenya will not feel free until the last traces of Colonialism and racial domination have been finally wiped out. We have in mind here the racial discrimination and brutalities of the South African régime. We deplore the oppressive measures of the Portuguese in Angola and Mozambique. And we are appalled by the contempt for democracy shown by the minority government of Southern Rhodesia, which is approaching tyrannical seizure of power by suppressing the will of the people.

In these matters, we look forward with confidence to more realistic support from the new Government in the United Kingdom. We especially anticipate that, in the case of Southern Rhodesia, a solution based on human equality will be found. Indeed, this will have to be found.

The future of Africa depends less on complex ideologies than on simple human values. Here, Kenya is a lesson for all. We are ourselves a kind of United Nations in miniature. And here all our citizens have equal respect; all have equal rights and responsibilities, and equal obligations, under the law.

One great imbalance within the United Nations structure springs from the exclusion of the People's Republic of China. The participation of China in the exchanges and activities of the United Nations is vital for lasting world peace. There is no other world forum in which conflicts, suspicions and injustices can be dissolved, by those dedicated through a Charter to the brotherhood of man.

Beyond its great purpose in political philosophy and adjustment, we in Kenya appreciate very greatly the practical efforts and aid of the United Nations, through its specialized agencies in the field. I well recall, in July last year, opening the Nairobi Office of the Technical Assistance Board and Special Fund. And I must assure Doctor Chidzero today how grateful we are for many forms of technical assistance offered by these bodies.

The foundation of Kenya's foreign policy is the principle of non-alignment. Our judgment is an independent judgment, not subject to power-bloc pressure or appeal. We have been working closely with the other member States of the Organization of African Unity. We have contributed to the activities and recommendations of the Afro-Asian bloc. In all our work and attitudes, we have sought to bring to our support for the United Nations a real commitment for peace and the social advancement of all mankind.

In our domestic concerns, and in our views on international disputes, we have deplored the argument of force. Kenya believes that the best way of resolving differences is by frank negotiation and discussion.

Human will in the context of world understanding must be rooted in a love of peace and an urge for human progress. We are therefore alarmed and discouraged, at times, when the so-called Great Powers pour out their treasure in fashioning greater and more horrifying weapons of destruction, while more and more other Powers seek to join the nuclear race.

Within the United Nations, we must work for the elimination of all these engines of destruction. We must seek the harnessing of nuclear energy for the peaceful purposes of mankind. And we must seek the allocation of all this astronomical finance to meet the real human challenges of hunger and ill-health and economic frustration.

Let the United Nations rule and secure that, on the threshold of the Space Age, our own shrinking planet should become a place of dignity and hope for all the human race.

Africa will be proud—Kenya will be proud—to make a contribution to this purpose. Let the twentieth year of this world body herald for all people a new era: absence of discrimination, opportunity for social progress, and freedom from fear.

AND during this contemporary period, the world lost two of its greatest leaders of our modern times. In a moving tribute in the House of Representatives, on November the 26th, 1963, the Prime Minister referred to the death of President John Kennedy of the United States, an event in Dallas, Texas, that had shocked mankind:

The whole world was shocked by the assassination of President Kennedy.

In just over three years of his term of office, President Kennedy succeeded in impressing the world with his courage, dedication and wisdom. More than any other American President before him, he succeeded in creating a working relationship with other leaders in the effort to secure world peace. He won many friends and admirers in all corners of the earth for his dedication to world peace. While serving his own country's interests, he was courageous enough to recognize and even accept responsibility for the interest of other countries and the world at large.

In recent months, President Kennedy became in the eyes of the Negroes another Lincoln. He spoke out for civil rights, and challenged the conscience of the American people. He risked unpopularity and even political office to try and finalize what Lincoln had started. This is all the more reason why the whole of Africa must mourn his death. President Kennedy's death must be the biggest challenge that American bigotry and racial hypocrisy has ever faced.

At the United Nations, and on the question of Afro-American relations, President Kennedy will be remembered for his new and more enlightened policies and interests. And we in Kenya have an additional special reason to remember him: because of his generous interest in assisting our young boys and girls to study in America through the student airlift.

The world has lost a great man whose name shall be written among the great, and whose life will be an inspiration for many generations to come.

JUST six months later, the Prime Minister attended (May the 29th, 1964) a mourning ceremony in Nairobi for the late Jawaharlal Nehru, the leader of India, whose death left world counsels the poorer. Jomo Kenyatta paid tribute in these words:

We have assembled today to mourn for a friend we held so dear.

Until his death a few days ago, Jawaharlal Nehru was known to the world as a champion of freedom and justice for all. It was his love for peace, and his uncompromising belief in the rights of man, that won him the admiration of many millions of people. It is not merely India that has lost a great leader and statesman, but the whole world.

Our sympathies go to his bereaved family, and to all the people of India. His body is dead, but his name will live forever, as one who loved his fellow-countrymen and those outside the country he led.

We are here to pray that he may rest in peace, and that the thoughts which he cherished should continue to inspire those of us who remain alive. Although we mourn in sorrow over his death, we can rejoice that his life and work were like a mirror reflecting the best in mankind.

7

Back to the Land

A MID all the commitments and cares of this period, both domestic and international, no single characteristic can really be said to have distinguished—in a phrase—either his policies or the Prime Minister himself: but if some single attribute had perforce to be selected, this might quite appropriately be his attachment to the soil of Kenya, his affinity with the land. Being a farmer ... talking farming ... these were the things that, by his own admission, Jomo Kenyatta liked to do. Presentation of this aspect, both of the Prime Minister and of the country's progress, may start with his 'Back to the Land' speech—a stern and serious speech—delivered over the television network on September the 11th, 1964:

Over the past few weeks, I have spoken at public meetings and called on our people to recognize the value of land. I have also urged our people to begin to dirty their hands in the effort of nation building.

Since Independence, the Government has kept in constant review the need for rapid economic growth, and for short term measures to secure relief of unemployment. All along, the Government has been aware that its first task in the effort to fulfil the aspirations of the people would be to accelerate the rate of economic growth.

So far, we have made an impressive start. But I would like today to discuss the part that the people themselves must play. It is not possible for our economic plans to succeed merely through Government measures and investment from overseas. Our greatest asset in Kenya is our land. This is the heritage we received from our forefathers. In land lies our salvation and survival. It was in this knowledge that we fought for the freedom of our country. Our plans for the future must spring from a resolve to put to maximum production our land, however small the acreage we may possess.

Our Party Manifesto contains proclamations and pledges which must guide our actions and decisions. A reference to it will show the importance attached to accelerating our agrarian revolution. It recognized that production of cash crops for the market constitutes the backbone of our economy. It called for a dynamic breakthrough in farming methods, to permit the financing of the Welfare State we intend to build.

In order to use our land efficiently and effectively, we must arrange that each farmer is sure of his land rights. We must also ensure that each farmer has the kind of security that would enable him to have access to necessary credit and loans, from Banks and other governmental and private agencies. Our Manifesto called for encouragement of land consolidation and registration of land titles, in order to facilitate these measures.

Anyone who has gone about the country will not fail to see the difference in development and production, as between areas where consolidation and new farming methods have been introduced, and areas where the old peasant methods are still in existence. Kenya has become a country governed by the normal pressures of a modern monetary economy. Land or cattle which do not yield enough income must be regarded as a liability, and a drain on our resources.

Many of our people have been attracted to the towns, and some believe that the only way of earning money is to work for wages and return to their land for brief visits. They leave their land unattended, or in the care of old mothers, wives or young brothers. This attitude is not only negative, but it promotes the biggest waste in Kenya today.

Many able-bodied people come to town and spend many months living on relatives and friends, and being generally a nuisance. Such people distort the purchasing power of their relatives and friends, making them poorer and miserable, and also interfere with the social plans and provisions for the genuine residents of the towns. This is a clear waste of manpower, and a definite obstacle to proper farming for the future. Any able-bodied man who exploits his relatives and friends in this manner is a disgrace to his manhood and to our society. Their friends and relatives must get rid of these people and stop feeding them.

Whereas we believe in African Socialism, we do not believe in loitering and laziness. We believe in co-operatives, but not in promoting a state of affairs in which some people try to live on the sweat of others.

The time for slogans and empty words has come to an end. We cannot cry for more land and yet fail to develop that which we have. The Government has shown its determination to fulfil its part. It has created political stability. It has introduced unemployment relief measures. It has stimulated and encouraged foreign investment. It has appealed to friends and received technical, financial and other help. It has produced a Development Plan, and thus defined the steps to be taken on the road towards prosperity.

It is now time for every citizen to make his contribution. We all agreed that Uhuru would mean hard work. We also agreed that progress would require sacrifice and discipline. Now, then, is the time to take the first step. We must begin from the base of our culture, the land. We must return to the land that we love. This is our greatest asset, and I now call on our people to complement the efforts and achievements of the Government in the last eight months, by exploiting to the full the soil of Kenya.

IF those words that he used were conclusions, Mzee Kenyatta had repeatedly given voice to his beliefs, and evidence for his findings. The first extract below is taken from a speech at Kigaari (August, 1964). This is followed by two extracts from a speech in the Machakos District (September, 1964):

Try to serve your country and to farm well, because all good things come from the soil.

*   *   *

I love the soil, and I love those who love the soil. You are my friends. The soil has knit us together . . . . It is our greatest investment. By investing in the soil, one invests in lasting, long-term property. Other things come and go, but well-cultivated soil remains. The soil has been there from the beginning of time . . . . Soil is the mother of wealth, development and general prosperity.

*   *   *

My theme today is: 'return to the soil'. You have made a good choice here, in rearing cows, goats and poultry. I myself go to my office every day. But I visit my shamba every day before going to the office. I do my garden work there. Maybe I cut a banana tree, or do some planting, or decide that the grass should be trimmed. I go back to the soil every morning of my life. I also see my poultry, and the few cows that produce enough milk for my household, and look at my sheep.

WHEN he opened the Elgeyo-Marakwet County Show at Kamarin— January the 10th, 1964—the Prime Minister offered full support to 'all progressive farmers':

My Government is strongly in support of all progressive farmers in this country, of whatever race, and my Government will do everything possible to help farmers with loans so that they can develop their farms. The Government will also help farmers to transport their crops, and help them look for markets, because without markets our products will be useless.

AND in a speech to a Coffee Co-operative at Kiambu—on August the 29th, 1964—he issued one of many calls to 'return to the land':

There are those who used to say that education was an end in itself. They held only one view of education: that it was a means of enabling a man to make money. But to make money, we must return to the land. It is often laughable to see a man with some acres of land going off to the town to seek employment, sometimes for a hundred shillings a month as a cook. If a man can effectively cultivate his own farm, it can prevent him being dependent on employers. What you want to do is return to the land . . . . If you do not concentrate on the land, future generations will call you unworthy, for having left nothing behind.

OPENING Kenya's principal Agricultural Show in Nairobi (September the 30th) gave the Prime Minister opportunity to deliver a complete review of agricultural policy. Placing the country's agricultural future in its true perspective, he spoke of plans for the expansion of many crops—some with irrigation—and of livestock industries. Then he categorized the farmer, as a man who was bound to enjoy both inward satisfaction and outward respect:

It gives me very great pleasure that I have been asked to open the Kenya Agricultural Show of 1964. I feel this pleasure not only because I am the first Prime Minister of an independent Kenya to be in this position, but also because I am myself a farmer. I therefore understand the importance which the Show has for the agricultural community, and indeed for all the people of Kenya.

Agriculture is the basis on which the whole economy rests. The Government can and will promote industrial expansion, but we recognize that unless this industrial expansion rests on a sound and broadly based agricultural industry, we cannot succeed in our task of creating greater wealth for our people.

I have been particularly pleased to see the exhibits put forward by the younger generation. It is vital to us that the youth of this country should be brought up to realize that agriculture is an honourable and satisfying occupation.

Young Farmers' Clubs deserve the fullest support, and I hope more and more farmers will give their time voluntarily to help these movements, because they provide a wonderful opportunity for our youth to get closer to the knowledge of the soil.

In the past year, agriculture has faced some difficulties. The coffee surplus has led to a system of quotas being imposed on all producing countries. At the present moment, our production is approximately 45,000 tons annually, but there are many young trees which have not yet come to maturity. From the trees already in the ground, we expect a crop of 70,000 tons by 1970.

The Government is determined to press our case for an increased quota, to assure the sale of coffee from existing plantings, and—if possible—to reach a position where we may encourage the planting of an increased acreage. Meanwhile, it is of the greatest importance that everyone engaged in the coffee industry should concentrate on improving standards of culture, picking and processing, so that we can preserve the highest standards of quality.

In this past year, the tea industry has seen considerable expansion. My Government has only recently signed a further agreement providing finance for the planting of an additional 14,000 acres of tea by 1970. Again, in order that this scheme may be successful, it is essential that the highest standards should be maintained.

While large new schemes of development always attract attention, the greatest immediate increase in production which can be obtained by the farmer will come from increased yields of all crops through the practice of basic good husbandry. By this I mean early land preparation, early planting, use of farmyard manure and fertilizers, early weeding, control of pests and diseases, and proper storage methods. Advice on all these matters can be obtained from the Government extension service.

Irrigation schemes will bring new land under cultivation, thus easing our unemployment problem. They will also generate more money to provide schools, hospitals and other necessary facilities. I believe that successful irrigation schemes will play a key role in our future development.

As to the livestock industry, a United Nations Special Fund survey team has started work in East Africa, to prepare a report on how this important section of agriculture should be developed. The survey will be completed about nine months hence, and will show how the livestock industry can be integrated in the three countries of East Africa. With the assistance of the report, we hope to be able to raise large sums of money from bodies such as the World Bank. Our aim will be to use the vast reservoir of stock existing in our pastoral areas to develop the ranchlands, so that they can carry more beasts to the acre, and thus to ensure that our valuable beef herds are maintained. If we can succeed in rearing the animals necessary to maintain a high-grade beef industry, we can raise additional foreign exchange from this source.

At the same time, we must not forget our valuable dairy herd. In the high potential areas of Kenya, we must make certain that our dairy stock is of the highest quality. In this way, we can ensure that our dairy production is economic, and that we can supply our own needs and have a substantial surplus for export at competitive prices.

No farming enterprise can flourish if the farmer is constantly threatened with the theft of his livestock and crops. The Government will take the strongest action against cattle and stock thieves.

My Government and I are fully alive to the need to ensure that Kenya, and all the undeveloped countries of the world, receive fair prices for their agricultural exports. I believe that it cannot be right for the prices we obtain for these exports to fluctuate so widely, in a world in which the cost of manufactured goods from the developed countries is steadily increasing.

It is necessary for the developed countries of the world to recognize our difficulties, and for a plan to be drawn up under which the prices for our agricultural exports will keep in step with increasing prices for those manufactured goods which we need to import to keep our economy buoyant.

Many of the unemployed have today got their ideas confused. There are vast areas of Kenya which are still undeveloped agriculturally, and no able-bodied man who has access to any undeveloped land should be seeking work in the towns. There is more than enough for this sort of person to do in developing agriculture. As a farmer, he will have greater respect from his fellows; he will be doing a better job for Kenya; and he will have a more satisfactory life.

I have the greatest faith in the farmer, and in his desire to see agriculture prosper. This Show is visible proof of what can be done by farmers who are dedicated to their work. Let everyone follow their example.

MANY times throughout this era, Mzee Kenyatta outlined to an audience the Government's plans for particular crops or new projects, calling—at the same time—for hard work and a greater grasp of modern farming technology. At a Kiambu ceremony on August the 29th, 1964:

Between now and 1970, we hope to expand the African production of sisal by 20,000 acres. Through settlement schemes, Government proposes to expand our pyrethrum exports by 50 per cent. by 1970.

The annual income from cotton is expected to be approximately £4½ million, which will make cotton Kenya's sixth most important commodity.

At the moment, we import 180,000 tons of sugar, and produce only 40,000 tons. The Government intends to accelerate sugar production so that our local supply will be able to satisfy our local demand by 1970.

I cannot tell you too strongly that all the Government's plans for agriculture finally depend on the co-operation, hard work and devotion of each one of you, to the cause of a free and independent and prosperous Kenya. Without hard work, nothing can be achieved.

The Government provides, through its Agricultural and Veterinary Departments, advice of the highest standard which is available to all of you without cost. This advice must be listened to and acted upon.

In addition, the Government is now spending some £200,000 per annum on subsidizing phosphate fertilizers. Every farmer must try to understand how these fertilizers can improve his yields, so that he gets the best possible crops from his farm. Without the will to help ourselves, we cannot succeed in our endeavours, no matter how much financial assistance we get from other countries.

*   *   *

My Government is facing the issue of coffee very realistically. Simply to say that the planting of coffee should be restricted denies to newcomers an opportunity to enter the coffee market. A more logical approach would be to let established coffee planters remove a certain proportion of their trees, thus enabling newcomers to plant a corresponding number. This would give meaning to the concept of equality.

AND at an opening ceremony at Mataara (October the 8th, 1964), the Prime Minister concentrated on the revolutionary scheme in Kenya for production of smallholder tea:

This factory . . . (the Mataara Tea Factory) . . . is the third in the long line of seventeen new factories, to be built for the processing of tea under the Kenya Tea Development Authority's programme. Funds to support this planting programme have come from the Kenya Government, the Commonwealth Development Corporation, and West Germany.

By 1970, the Government expects to spend over £2 million in order to extend the total tea acreage from 50,000 to 75,000 acres. The target value of Kenya's tea production will then be about £11 million. The scheme for planting tea by smallholders in Kenya is one of the most imaginative and ambitious smallholder schemes in the world.

I am pleased to hear of the interest which growers are taking in the work of the Kenya Tea Development Authority, through meetings of divisional, district and regional Tea Committees and Boards. In this way, individual growers become united with others of common interest, in working for the success of the scheme as a whole.

The policies laid down by the Authority with regard to planting, cultivation and pruning, and encouraging the use of fertilizers, have one aim only: to help the grower to increase the yield of green leaf from his 'shamba'.

An integral part of this great scheme is the programme of factory construction, which is being undertaken on a partnership basis. This factory at Mataara—which has cost over £100,000—is financed by means of loan and share capital subscribed by the Commonwealth Development Corporation, Arbuthnot Latham and Company, and Dalgety (East Africa) Ltd. In this way, practical know-how is allied with overseas finance in the interests of Kenya's development.

From the very outset it has been the intention to invite growers, or their representatives, to join in the ownership of the factory, and a special block of shares is set aside to be issued for this purpose. Furthermore, it is specifically stated in the finance agreement between the existing partners that, once the loans have been repaid, the entire holdings of shares can be sold to growers.

I hope that growers will take this opportunity—offered to them now—to become part-owners of this fine factory. And during the coming years, they have special reason to do all they can to help this factory company to succeed, in the knowledge that one day the factory can belong to them entirely.

WITHIN the whole content of agriculture—planned production and efficient marketing—the Prime Minister made it known at all times that he placed great reliance on the increasing role of the co-operative movement, in meeting many problems that had to be resolved to assure the development of Kenya. At Kiambu (August the 29th, 1964), at a foundation-stone ceremony, he first praised a local—and substantial—co-operative enterprise, and then outlined certain of the Government's plans for co-operative expansion:

I am sure that the existence of this impressive building . . . (new Headquarters of the Kiambu Coffee Growers' Co-operative Union) . . . will demonstrate to all the ability of our people to manage their own affairs in an independent Kenya. It will also show the ability of our African farmers to increase most rapidly their direct participation in agriculture, Kenya's most vital industry.

As a farmer, I have followed with interest the progress you have made. It gives me satisfaction today to know that you have a Co-operative Union consisting of ten Societies and 11,000 members. Your 24 factories are a fine example of co-operation and initiative, while the expected turnover of £500,000 from your 13,000 acres point to the profits awaiting those like yourselves who have decided to concentrate on the land.

I would like to tell you some intentions of my Government in regard to co-operatives. The Ministry of Commerce and Industry is preparing legislation to strengthen—in various ways—its powers and functions, and those of the Commissioner of Co-operative Development. Among the more important provisions will be the granting of powers to the Commissioner to control Societies, so that he may prevent the establishment of too many weak Societies.

At the present time, there are some 540 Co-operative Societies of all types, with a yearly turnover approaching £30 million. Many of these, however, are very small and lacking in the essential strength so necessary for progress. It is Government's intention, wherever possible and appropriate, that as many crops as possible will be handled by one Society, instead of having a separate Society for each crop. This will mean bigger and stronger Societies. You will appreciate that the larger the Society, the better it can afford to engage suitably qualified staff to ensure that its affairs are run properly.

We intend to foster a Kenya Federation of Co-operatives, to unite all registered Societies, and to represent the co-operative movement whenever necessary. The Federation would be an advisory body in its early stages, and we would hope that it would be able to offer substantial help and advice, particularly to the smaller co-operative units.

The Government intends, at the national and lower levels, to provide suitable training. A total sum of £44,000 per annum has been earmarked to provide this training by 1970. It is hoped that, by then, the co-operative movement will have become entirely self-supporting.

WHEN he opened Kenya's largest co-operative farming unit—in Machakos District—on September the 5th, 1964, the Prime Minister seized the opportunity to offer further encouragement to co-operative ventures of many kinds:

This is a co-operative farm registered as the Drumvale Farmers Co-operative Society Limited. There are 75 members of this Society, and between them they have raised £23,000 for their half-share in the purchase price of the farm.

This is a lot of money for ordinary people to produce, and it reflects great credit on the energy and persistence of all the members of this Society that they should have been able to find it. Having raised it, they then had to get a loan from the Land Bank and from the Agricultural Finance Corporation, and this they have succeeded in doing. They now have a first-class farm of nearly 8,000 acres, going in for dairy and poultry production and ranching. It is producing 350 gallons of milk per day, and nearly 300 eggs, and although no cattle have as yet been sold, something like 200 will be ready for sale in a few months time.

With such a splendid start, I am quite certain that this Society will develop and expand, until they have one of the best farms of its type in Kenya. The Drumvale Farmers Co-operative is easily the biggest co-operative farming unit we have at the moment, and it will provide an example for very many.

Twelve other Societies, all of them smaller than this, have already purchased farms, and between them have been given loans by the Land Bank amounting to over £70,000. A total of about 90 co-operative farming societies have now been registered by the Commissioner for Co-operative Development, and I understand there is a waiting list of about 80 more which have still to be registered. Clearly, the movement towards co-operative farming can and must succeed, and my Government will do all in its power to help.

Our efforts will be useless, however, unless you—the individual farmers and members of these co-operatives—do your utmost to succeed. There is no more important task in Kenya at the moment than that of developing the land and making it productive. This can only be done if people like yourselves work hard, and learn as fast as you can from whoever is willing to teach you.

We also hope to see a great expansion in co-operative work arising from our settlement schemes, and we want to develop a wide range of rural industries based on Co-operative Societies.

Some work on these lines has already been done. A group of women, for example—at Kipipiri settlement scheme on the Kinangop—quite recently had samples of dyed cloth on display in the Art Gallery of the New Stanley Hotel. This cloth was bought by visitors to Kenya, and will help to spread abroad a good picture of Kenya and its people, and the sort of things they are able to do.

AND then, at the opening of yet another Coffee Co-operative factory—at Gatanga on October the 10th, 1964—Jomo Kenyatta spoke of the meaning and value of co-operative principles. Calling for high standards of management, he promised Government aid of many kinds for a national co-operative organization:

Societies such as yours . . . (Gatanga Coffee Growers' Co-operative Society) . . . demonstrate what can be accomplished through the growth of the co-operative movement in Kenya. They show what can be achieved when individual efforts are pooled together in a Co-operative Society, and organized effectively to accomplish specific economic objectives.

The co-operative movement is, by its very nature, a means of fulfilling our goals of economic growth and African socialism. Co-operatives build upon the traditional values and foundations of our society, transforming these values into effective economic and social institutions.

Through the co-operative movement, each farmer and small trader can participate in the development of Kenya. Through the co-operative movement we can pull together, to increase our production of food, to improve our marketing of crops, and to improve the distribution of goods and services throughout the economy.

We can do this, and yet at the same time—through the co-operative principles of one member, one vote; distribution of surpluses on the basis of participation, not ownership; and limitation of the power of capital—build a society which is free from exploitation.

We want to build in Kenya an independent, self-supporting co-operative movement. We do not intend to do all your work for you, but intend to work with you to make the co-operative movement strong and healthy. We are willing to do our share, but it is up to you to do your share as well. For example, it is up to you as members to elect honest Committee members, to set high standards for the management of your affairs, and to make sure that your Managers live up to these high standards.

There are today too many Co-operative Societies which are too small. These Societies depend on our Government Inspectors to keep their books. Frequently, they are too small to do a good job for their members.

We want these small Societies to join together with other Societies, so that they can become effective economic organizations, able to do their job on the scale that is required. We want to build strong District Unions, to co-ordinate co-operative development within each District, and to provide centralized services to the primary Societies which are its members.

We want to build the co-operative movement at the national level by encouraging the Kenya National Federation of Co-operatives to become an effective organization. This is a brief outline of our plans to build a new structure of co-operation in Kenya.

I am happy to be able to announce today that preliminary steps are now being taken to form a Co-operative Bank in Kenya. I am also happy to say that the local commercial Banks have given us assurances that they fully support this project, and will be willing to give us every possible assistance in establishing the Bank and helping to train its staff. This help from the commercial Banks is very welcome, and very much appreciated.

Many of the existing Co-operative Societies, as well as new Societies, have been raising funds to purchase farms. It is difficult for one African to buy a large-scale farm in the former European areas, but the pooling of resources through a Co-operative can often make this possible.

This is a vital contribution of the co-operative movement, as it is important to the future of Kenya that these farms remain intact. We will do all we can to enable Co-operative Societies, irrespective of their size, to continue the process of buying farms.

I have been assured by the Minister for Commerce and Industry that regulations have now been formulated, to make sure that if—unfortunately—a Society should fail, then the farm it has purchased will not be divided among the members. The deed to the farm, after all, is not in the names of individual members, but in the name of the Society. The farm will remain intact as it was before.

THE problem to which the Prime Minister referred at Gatanga—that of keeping in being as economic units some of the larger scale farms—was frequently in his mind. In a Machakos speech (September, 1964), he said this:

We have heard a lot in Kenya lately about the problems we shall face if we break up big farms in order to make a lot of little farms. This is a very real problem, because in many cases the big farms can only produce efficiently if they remain reasonably big. I know that—in many cases and in many places in Kenya—it is possible to run a very small farm, perhaps only ten or twenty acres, quite efficiently, and contribute fully to the country's economy, but I know also that very often this cannot be done. Frequently, the farm has to be retained as a big one.

Lately, we have had references in the world press to the problems we are facing in agriculture in Kenya. Some of these reports have tried to give a very unhappy picture of developments in Kenya, particularly stressing our difficulties over the settlement of our people on large farms. Of course, there is a very great problem here, and we are very well aware of it. We know that there are many difficulties, and that we shall not succeed in developing our economy without great efforts.

A T the same time, Mzee Kenyatta was proud of the progress the country had made with resettlement projects, and announced with satisfaction at a public rally in Nairobi on June the 21st, 1964, that:

More than 60,000 people have been given land on settlement schemes, on land which used to belong to the settlers.

T HE Prime Minister took a personal interest—amid his other manifold duties—in the overall planning of resettlement, and in decisions affecting areas of particular difficulty. For example, on December the 4th, 1963, following the return of a Kenya delegation from London, he said:

The Colonial Secretary, Mr. Duncan Sandys, recently informed the House of Commons that the British Government was willing to provide additional funds, to meet a difficult and urgent situation in mixed farming areas of the Central Region, where landlessness and unemployment are particularly severe.

Subsequently, a Kenya Government delegation led by the Minister for Agriculture, Mr. Bruce McKenzie, has discussed with the British authorities steps necessary to solve this problem. It has been agreed that, as a first priority and subject to a practicable scheme being worked out, land in the Ol Kalou salient should be made available for African occupation during 1964.

There are other areas, particularly to the north and north-west of Nyeri, where there is likely to be an equally pressing problem. We shall consider this with the British Government when the general position is reviewed in a few months' time.

This means that, during 1964, practically the whole of the land in Nyandarua will be Africanized. I wish to assure those landless Africans who did not get plots of land during the present crash settlement programme that they will have the opportunity of obtaining plots as soon as more land is acquired in Nyandarua.

L ATER—at a news conference in Nairobi on August the 12th, 1964—Jomo Kenyatta followed up his earlier announcement with details of new settlement arrangements in this zone. He also referred to continuing negotiations with Britain which will affect a further two million acres of mixed farming land:

The British Government has today agreed to provide the Kenya Government with £1½ million, partly by loan and partly by gift, to enable European farms in the Ol Kalou salient, and in the Dundori-Bahati areas, to be purchased and Africans to be settled on the land.

The Dundori–Bahati farms, consisting of approximately 10,000 acres, will be sub-divided and used as a high-density settlement scheme. This should accommodate about 3,000 people.

The remainder of the Ol Kalou salient, approximately 140,000 acres, will be purchased at prices based on current profitability, and will be farmed without sub-division: in some instances by putting the present farms together to make a single unit, and through farming practices such as co-operatives.

I warn farmers in the area that those properties which have continued to be farmed well will most certainly get a fair price. Those farms which have been abandoned, mismanaged or partially run down will get much lower prices, as a certain element of the finance will be needed to rehabilitate such farms. This warning has been consistently given by my Government, and especially by the Minister for Agriculture, and we are now taking action as promised.

This take-over will mean that at least 20,000 people will be involved in moving into a new life. Announcements on the method of choosing settlers will be made shortly, but priority will be given to genuine existing employed labour on the farms.

Further discussions are still going on with the British Government over the purchase of the remaining mixed farms owned by Europeans who do not wish to remain in Kenya. The basis of our discussion is to take over these farms within a suitable given period of time. Care will be taken, while doing so, not to affect the great value of the farms to the national economy.

The acreage of land in question is around two million acres, which will accommodate 200,000 families, or about a million people. It is hoped that we shall be able to make an announcement of the results of our discussions later this year.

8

Realities of Economic Life

APART from the paramount need to generate new production and higher yields in a primarily agricultural country, the Prime Minister was faced at the outset with overall responsibility for economic reconstruction: the need for industrial expansion; the consequent need for large-scale investment; the accompanying need for local participation in economic growth; problems of capital resources, and power resources, and shortage of skilled manpower, and widespread unemployment among untrained men. When he opened the new Oil Refinery at Changamwe on February the 21st, 1964, Mzee Jomo Kenyatta covered some of this ground—investment; training schemes; the need for diversity in industry:

It was with great pleasure that I accepted the invitation to open this oil refinery here in Mombasa. It is the first oil refinery in this part of the African Continent, and I am glad that Kenya has become the first country on the whole of the eastern side of Africa to have so important an industry.

When you consider the contribution that this oil refinery will make to the saving of our foreign exchange, to our employment opportunities, and—if I may say so—to our Government Treasury, you will no doubt agree with me that this is another milestone in our economic advancement.

This, I am sure, will act as an additional source of encouragement to potential investors, because they will realize that Kenya can and does support a modern, highly-automated and complex industry.

Another thing which has impressed me forcibly is that it has become possible, from the outset, to fill so many responsible posts with local people whom you have trained, and who have a very bright future in this industry.

A great deal of money has been spent on the building of this refinery, and I should like to take this opportunity to repeat what I have said before, regarding our intention to continue attracting and welcoming foreign investment here.

I believe it must by now be absolutely clear to everyone that my

Government actively wishes to encourage more and more investment from all countries. We are striving to develop our country in accordance with our own independent policies, and we shall not tolerate seeing Kenya become just another industrial or commercial protege of any foreign country, or any power bloc from anywhere.

We in Kenya have played our part in the past, and we shall continue to play our part, in accelerating capital accumulation. And we are determined to accelerate economic growth within the context of African Socialism, meaning that both the Government and private enterprise will have a contribution to make.

I am fully aware of the fact that Companies such as this one find it necessary to employ not only the local people, but also some experts from overseas. I want these experts to feel welcome in this country. I am sure they will contribute their best to make this refinery a success, and to increase the skill of our people.

I do not know to what extent it is planned that this refinery should go in for the manufacture of other chemicals in the process of refining, but I understand that there is a surprising range of such chemicals, and that they could have great importance in the development of related secondary industries.

I have just been given the first instalment of a gift by the East African Oil Refineries to the National Fund which will total £20,000. This gift is for the support of the Small Industries Training Centre to be established by the Kenya Government at Nakuru.

We often hear public statements regarding the setting up of big Companies, both in Kenya and in other countries in Africa, and this always sounds impressive. But there must also be many smaller industries, systematically developed on as large a scale as possible.

I was very proud when, two or three months ago, my attention was drawn to a radio manufacturing Company in Kenya wholly owned and run by Africans. There are several other similar firms in existence, and we plan to expand the present twenty or so such small industries to a total—over the next few years—of three or four hundred, with an annual output of over £1½ million in value.

This oil refinery is itself a product of great scientific technical skill, business foresight, and confidence in our future.

THE need for maintaining confidence, as the bulwark of investment, was constantly in the Prime Minister's mind. In Parliament (July, 1963), and in Nairobi (June, 1964), he said:

It is the duty of the Government to create confidence, so that people from abroad will want to invest their money in this country.

*   *   *

Already, because of harmony and goodwill, investors are bringing in more capital. With increased investment here, we shall be able to educate our children.

A ND then, speaking in Nairobi on June the 10th, 1964, the Prime Minister launched the country's new and comprehensive six-year Development Plan. He emphasised that any modern economy must demand full contribution from all:

The Development Plan predicts that the economy will grow rapidly to yield £360 million a year by 1970. Each of our 1,800,000 families will then have an average income of £200, despite the increase of 400,000 families .... Modern economy demands that everyone should contribute to development. Farmers must develop every acre of their holdings; workers must increase their productivity; investors and commercial firms must continue to show confidence in our country; civil servants and defence forces must work diligently and loyally. I appeal to all citizens to join hands with the Government, in the spirit of 'harambee', in a new and exciting stage of nation-building.

O N September the 29th, 1964, Mzee Kenyatta delivered a major speech to an assembly of businessmen in the Nairobi City Hall. On this occasion, the Prime Minister dealt with Kenya's commercial expansion; he defined the Government's purpose in establishing a mixed economy; he spoke of means of ensuring African integration in business; and he assured private investors that they need not fear nationalization:

When we became a sovereign nation last year, my Government gave an assurance that the conditions necessary for accelerated growth would continue to be maintained and improved. This assurance was addressed as much to the business community as to the agricultural community, because we recognized these are but separate branches of the same nation.

In order to achieve our aim, we decided to spread our commercial and trade contacts to countries with whom these activities had hitherto been either non-existent or negligible. Apart from the need to spread marketing risks, this step also suited our approach to international problems. We believe in a policy of non-alignment in foreign affairs.

When we choose some techniques from the East, it is not because we approve the conduct of their domestic or foreign policies; nor should we be accused of being pro-West if we adopt or perpetuate some Western ideas. We are determined to develop Kenya as a democratic African Socialist country.

As a result of trade agreements concluded with many socialist countries of Europe and Asia, we have increased the volume of our external trade considerably. At the same time, we have maintained and increased our trade in our traditional markets.

We have been anxious, together with other like-minded nations, to stress the importance of a more liberal attitude towards the importation of primary products from developing countries. In this connection, the immediate results of the Geneva Conference were disappointing; but I would like to express the hope that, in the long term, tariff walls and quota systems will be brought to a more reasonable level.

I have stated before, and I wish to repeat, that our aim is to establish a mixed economy. And I would like to dispel the confusion which seems to surround this objective. By a mixed economy, we mean that we shall work towards a situation in which the role of private enterprise and that of Government are complementary to each other. Here, Government realizes that Africans must be integrated in the commercial and industrial life of the nation. We are therefore instituting measures which will enable Africans to play an ever-increasing part in these fields.

But we are determined that the development of African business and industries should be carried out without damaging the existing fabric of the economy. A simple transfer of a business from one man to another does not necessarily expand business or develop a country. Some machinery already exists for this purpose, but we propose to set up additional organizations. I am thinking of the Industrial and Commercial Development Corporation, and the Development Finance Company, through which the Kenya Government will directly participate in industrial projects in partnership with private capital.

One of the greatest weaknesses in our commerce is that, in the distributive trade, it is not always easy for the small retailers to get reliable service from wholesalers. In this sector, we need the commercial equivalent of land consolidation. We consider that the most efficient way of achieving this 'commercial consolidation' is to develop a State-owned Company, which will act as a focal point for reorganising and expanding the distributive trade.

We also consider that, in order to derive maximum benefits from our agreements for mutual trade with the socialist countries, it is necessary to establish a single State-controlled Agency. I must emphasise here that it is not the intention to swamp the distributive trade by a monolithic Government organization, and there must remain a very large section of the economy under private enterprise.

A similar approach will be adopted for industrial projects which the Government may find it necessary to initiate. You know that up till now, industrial development has been sponsored by private enterprise. But we have reached a stage where certain enterprises can only be launched if they are financially backed by Government.

You must not interpret my remarks as implying nationalization. We consider that nationalization will not serve to advance the cause of African Socialism.

You will appreciate that we have gone to greater pains to guarantee private investment than most countries have done. The Constitution provides safeguards for private property. In addition to these, the Government has provided further safeguards in the proposed Foreign Investments (Protection) Bill. Our taxation system, including investment allowances, offers further testimony of our determination to assist. I urge you, therefore, to study this Act, and reassure your associates overseas that it is the Government's intention, not only to continue to work together with private enterprise, but also to promote conditions in which private enterprise can thrive. In this connection, Government will continue the policy of tariff protection for pioneer and infant industries, including refunds of custom duty for imported raw materials.

If we have confidence in each other, if the business community understands Government's problems, and the Government understands your problems, then we can develop and build up this country to become a real force in Africa and in the world.

IN the course of this same speech, the Prime Minister dwelt particularly—at one stage—on the problem of unemployment in Kenya, and the means that must be sought and found for meeting a shortage of skilled personnel to implement the Development Plan:

At home, one of the very pressing problems is that of unemployment. I wish to assure you how much my Government appreciates the co-operation which private employers have given in our endeavour to find a solution. I refer to the Tripartite Agreement, under which private employers agreed to take on additional labour. I regard this as the true manifestation of the spirit of 'harambee'.

But we fully realise that a long-term solution can only be found by the achievement of a more rapid economic development, which would create increased employment opportunities.

In the past, we have been more fortunate than most African countries in possessing a reservoir of skilled manpower, which has been an important factor in attracting investment. However, I am advised that, if the economy continues to expand as fast as it is doing, we shall be running into a shortage of skilled personnel. We shall need people not only to tighten nuts and bolts, but also to make precision instruments. To fill this gap, Government has placed high priority on secondary school education, particularly in its technical and scientific fields, in the six-year Development Plan.

I know that the private businessman is already playing a major role in the development of our nation. But I would like to appeal to you to consider all possible schemes for training your staff, to enable us to meet our future needs for skilled manpower.

DURING the previous month—at a news conference in Nairobi on August the 19th, 1964—Jomo Kenyatta outlined some of the measures that the Government was taking to alleviate unemployment. He then emphasised that a general expansion of the economy could be the only long term answer:

It has been stated on many occasions by the Kenya Government that the engagement of its additional workers under the Tripartite Agreement . . . (an Agreement between the Employers' Federation, the Federation of Labour, and Government, as a means of tackling the unemployment problem) . . . is a complex matter. This is so because it is necessary for the projects on which the workers are engaged to be blended in with Government's long term programmes under the national Development Plan. The several projects which will enable Government's full quota to be engaged require varying periods of planning, and their commencement dates are greatly dependent on the availability of finance, specialist staff, plant, equipment and materials.

It is once again emphasized that there is no relaxation in the

Government's efforts to meet its quota under the Tripartite Agreement. To this end, efforts are now being made to take on more workers under the following schemes:

(*a*) The Government has just acquired the Rifle Range Camp for the National Youth Service, and recruitment of the first intake began last Friday. By the middle of September, 500 youths will be taken on;

(*b*) This week, the Ministry of Lands and Settlement has engaged 500 workseekers from Nairobi, and the Ministry of Agriculture 200, to be given jobs at various places;

(*c*) Discussions have taken place between the Government and the Nairobi City Council, for the Council to employ—on behalf of the Government—part of its quota under the Tripartite Agreement;

(*d*) The Ministry of Agriculture has plans to employ—within the next few weeks—at least 650 workers from many places. Recruitment of 200 men to be employed at the Veterinary Water Falls Estate is now in progress;

(*e*) At the Mwea-Tebere irrigation scheme, 300 workers will be taken on in the next week or two;

(*f*) Last week, 150 workers were taken on at the Estella Estate, which was an abandoned farm. Other such schemes involving 130 workers have been planned for immediate execution;

(*g*) Loans have already been given to Thika, Nakuru and Kisumu for building programmes, which means that more workers will be engaged by these Authorities;

(*h*) Central Government Ministries have been authorised to take on more staff, to enable the Government to meet its quota. At least 100 workseekers will be employed;

(*i*) The Ministry of Works has a number of projects on hand, some of which will start immediately. The recruitment of 500 men for construction of the Ulu to Sultan Hamud section of the Mombasa road is now nearly completed. This will be followed by further recruitment of about 700 men—about two months hence—for realignment of the Mombasa road on either side of Kibwezi;

(*j*) A further 100 men will be engaged by the Ministry of Works for building maintenance purposes.

In all these schemes, at least 4,510 workers will be employed.

I would like to make a strong appeal to all the registered workers not to go in large numbers to the Registration Offices. This does not make it easy for the Labour Officer handling this problem. Registered workseekers are advised to wait until they are called by the Labour Officers concerned.

I would also like to give a strong warning to those who are now being offered jobs. Reports have reached me that some people have tended to be choosy, and have rejected jobs offered them. Such people must be made aware that—when that happens—the Government will not make any more efforts to give them other jobs.

Finally, I would like to call for full co-operation by all parties concerned in this exercise. Those people who are agitating on this issue must realise that they are doing a great deal of harm to this country. My Government expects all people to be responsible, and such actions or statements as may compel the Government to take stern measures should be avoided.

Strikes and threats of strikes or lock-outs should be avoided completely during the life of the Tripartite Agreement. We should not allow ourselves to be carried away by emotion and agitation, to the extent that those already in employment will go on strike while their brothers are standing outside offices waiting to be placed in employment. This creates a very poor impression, both in and outside Kenya.

All the measures which the Government and industry have taken to alleviate unemployment can only be regarded as temporary. The long term solution of the problem is a general improvement of our economy. Our efforts must, therefore, be directed towards the long term measures which will give the country the necessary economic stability.

9

Education sets the Pace

A tremendous hunger for education has normally followed the attainment of Independence by many African States. Kenya proved to be no exception. This hunger comprised both an individual urge for literacy and learning, among the people themselves, and in respect of their children, and it was also measurable as a critical national need: the need to staff a developing country in all ranks of administration, commerce, technology and the professions. The Prime Minister touched on this latter point at the opening of the Chesamisi Secondary School in Elgon Nyanza, on August the 3rd, 1964:

My Government is well aware that, although facilities for secondary education have been increasing steadily for the past decade, there are insufficient places still for all the boys and girls who are able to benefit from some form of post-primary schooling. We are very concerned about the shortage of educational opportunities and, as you can see from the Development Plan which was recently announced, we are prepared to devote a very large part of our national resources for the next six years to education.

Everyone is earnestly endeavouring to play his part in ensuring that our young people are well educated, and that Kenya provides for them the professional, technical and commercial skills which they and our country need. The main foundation on which these skills will be built is secondary education. It is natural—and indeed essential—for our Government and people to concentrate their hopes and efforts on secondary education at this stage of our nation's advance towards a rich and rewarding life for all.

You will understand, though, that we cannot devote all our resources to education, and that even if we could, we should not be able to transform the situation overnight. We are determined to improve educational opportunities as rapidly as we can, but there are obvious limits to what we can do: limiting factors are money, buildings and equipment, and teachers.

We are determined, too, not only to provide more secondary education, but also to provide it in a variety of forms—academic, technical, commercial and vocational—and to see that it is of fine quality as well as increased quantity. To achieve this, we must establish no more schools than we can afford; we must not skimp on buildings and equipment; and we must secure—and ourselves train—an adequate supply of qualified teachers.

THEN, during a ceremony at the Githunguri Secondary School on October the 10th, 1964, Mzee Kenyatta stressed the need for educational planning, in order to make the best possible use of always-limited finance:

Self-help schemes must not be regarded as being in competition with what the Government is trying to do. The people of this country must accept the guidance and advice given by officials of the Ministry of Education. Unless this is done, then the country's education might be in jeopardy.

I would like to stress at this point the need for planning and control of our educational expansion. The vast majority of our people are working constantly to ensure an education for their children. This is good, but if these children go to bad schools, without adequate facilities and without good teachers, the kind of education they receive may not help them much in after life.

In order to ensure the provision of reasonable facilities, and the maintenance of good educational standards, it is essential to work out how the task of educating our children and of nation building must be undertaken. To this end, my Government has already taken very clear steps. Recognizing the importance of being self-dependent on our own educated and qualified people, the Government has placed the greatest priority on secondary education.

No stone will be left unturned to ensure as full a response as funds will permit to the educational aspirations of all Kenyans. Shortage of funds—as everyone would agree—is our greatest stumbling-block. We have the foresight and the initiative. We also have the will. But we have not had available all the funds needed to implement fully every aspect of our Development Plan. However, we both trust and believe that—through the spirit of 'harambee'—Kenya will go ahead.

Because many people fully appreciate the financial limitations facing our Government, and also through the sheer urge for self-help, there are now well over sixty unaided secondary schools in Kenya.

As I have already said, the spirit behind the establishment of such schools—of which Githunguri is one—is highly commendable.

The one point which may prove to be unfortunate about them is their rather large number, which in all probability will increase. Any attempt on the part of the Government to offer public aid to any one of them must be made with the clear understanding that the others will also have to be favourably considered.

APART from education at primary or secondary level, the hunger for study at undergraduate level—in the Arts and Sciences, and for such professions as Medicine, Engineering and Law—was also acute. So was the country's need for graduates in all these fields. Pending the creation and full development of the East African University, a stream of students left (or planned to leave) from Kenya to seek their higher education overseas. Occasionally, backbench or other comment associated this education with the political systems of host countries. Thus, in Parliament on July the 23rd, 1963, the Prime Minister felt bound to make this comment:

Some backbenchers have said our people must be trained in Ghana or in Cairo or in other African countries, not in imperialist or Western countries. Brothers, I want to assure you that knowledge is knowledge, irrespective of who gives it. You must make a distinction between knowledge and ideology. We do not send our people overseas to get the ideology of Britain or America or Russia. We send them to get knowledge, to come back to this country to help us work for our future.

Thousands of students from Ghana and Nigeria and other African countries go to America or Britain or Russia. They cannot all be accommodated in their own countries, so they go where they can be trained. We shall follow the same idea.

ON December the 13th, 1963, during the Uhuru celebrations, the Prime Minister was the central figure at an Academic Ceremony at the Royal College (now known as the University College, Nairobi). In his speech, he dealt with many of the principles of University work and purpose, including the maintenance of standards, and the application of these principles to modern East African needs:

It is a great honour that you bestow upon me in electing me an Honorary Fellow of this Royal College. It is an honour not only on my own behalf, but also on behalf of the people of Kenya. For I know that it has been given—in part—as an expression of rejoicing by the College at the birth of this new nation.

No country can gain, or retain, Independence worthy of the name, unless the life of that country is sustained by the knowledge and skill of its own citizens. The Royal College, during its short lifetime, has already made a great and valuable contribution to that store of knowledge, and that body of educated men and women needed in every sphere of our national life.

It has been a principal aim of the University of East Africa, since the beginning, to secure the deployment of University facilities in the three University Colleges in the most economical and effective way possible. The concentration of certain professional Schools in one or other of the Colleges has not only made possible a large financial saving, but has also promised the benefits of a larger-scale academic organization than dispersal would have allowed.

Thus, we in Kenya—in our Royal College—supply the entire needs of the University in Engineering, Commerce and Veterinary Science. And although we share these facilities with students from our neighbouring East African countries, I need not emphasize the advantage to us in Kenya of having these sources of trained manpower on our doorstep.

This measure of functional specialization has been brought about through recognition by the four countries of East Africa of their common interest, and of the advantages that co-operation can bring to them all. It also indicates their determination to maintain University standards at a level that is fully comparable with Universities all over the world. We need these standards, not only because nothing less is adequate for the requirements of East Africa, but also to ensure that our scholars have access to centres of specialised research and learning on an equal basis with scholars from other countries.

The Royal College—in common with Makerere College in Kampala and the University College of Dar es Salaam—has in the past depended to a large extent on overseas aid, both in money and in staff. It is with much gratification that I have heard of the continuing financial support that we have been promised from overseas, to enable us to put into effect the development plan for 1964-67.

I am also pleased to notice the prospect held out to us that, by 1967, some 40 per cent. of the academic staff—taking the three Colleges together—will be African. I am sure our European friends, and especially the present European members of the staff, will unite with me in approving such a change. It is necessary for our Independence that we should be increasingly self-sufficient in the higher reaches of research and learning.

At the same time, I want to take this opportunity to express my gratitude, and that of Kenya, for the very great help that overseas Professors and lecturers have given—and are continuing to give—in building up the human resources necessary for our Independence, our welfare and our progress.

SOME time afterwards—March the 10th, 1964—Jomo Kenyatta opened a new Veterinary School attached to the University. He used this occasion to reaffirm the importance that must be attached to technological training, and to the fashioning within East Africa of expert skills:

The Kenya Government is very grateful to the Rockefeller Foundation for its generosity to the Veterinary School . . . (the new Pre-Clinical Veterinary School of the University College, Nairobi) . . . and for presenting to the School this fine building in which we now stand. My Government also warmly welcomes the experts who have come to help the staff of this School from Universities in several countries, notably from Glasgow and Geissen.

The Government is glad to be assured that, with this magnificent help, the Veterinary School will be able to award a Degree of the highest standard. Thus, our University College in Nairobi will fulfil its responsibility—as part of the University of East Africa—to train Veterinary Officers and teachers for all East Africa, both to replace departing expatriates and to provide for the growing needs of East African agriculture, our most important industry.

In this way, the University College will show its ability to provide the technological training that East Africa needs, and which the College is also providing in its Schools of Engineering, Architecture, and related subjects. We already have here in Nairobi a more advanced and broadly-based technological complex than most young Capitals can boast, and many natural advantages.

East Africa's technologists require the skills of many more experts than we can hope to train for some time. We are therefore very glad that the University College should have attracted so many highly qualified teachers and experts, in many fields and from many countries, to Nairobi. We shall need all their help, and warmly welcome them in our midst.

10

Health and Social Welfare

'POVERTY, ignorance and disease ....' During and since the struggle for Independence in Kenya, these were the principal social evils cited by the Prime Minister and the Government as representing immediate challenge. Removing these evils, and their framework of social injustice, has been the main inspiration of the Government's work and planning. Mzee Kenyatta made frequent reference, throughout this period, to new hope for the needy and the sick, the destitute and the under-privileged. Following the opening by the Mayor of Nairobi of a new housing estate (July the 18th, 1963), he said this:

I am very happy to be here today, and to be taking part in this important occasion for the City Council and the people of Nairobi.

My Government is dedicated to work for the progress and prosperity of all the people of this country. In the forefront of our aims is determination to improve the living standards of our people.

One aspect—and a very important aspect—of improved living standards is the need to build more and better housing: not the provision of 'bed spaces' but the provision of homes, where the dignity of the individual can flourish, and where the family and all that is best in family life can thrive and prosper.

While it is true that it is men, not walls, that make a City, do not let us forget that so long as people are denied the basic needs of life, so long as they are compelled to struggle against hunger, disease, and lack of proper shelter, they cannot contribute to the making of a City. So not only are their efforts lost to us, but their dignity as human beings is impaired.

It is against this human indignity, wherever it is found and whatever its form, that my Government—in co-operation with Local Authorities, voluntary agencies, and every man and woman of goodwill—is pledged and determined to fight. It is because Ofafa Jericho represents a victory in that fight, as does the demolition of Kariokor, that I am so glad to be here today.

I congratulate the Nairobi City Council on this splendid project, and I am happy that the Government of Kenya has been associated with it. Here is a fine example of the spirit of 'harambee'. Here is an example also of the essential part in our affairs that is played by local government.

Local government provides not only an essential link between the people and the Central Government, but it offers to every citizen an opportunity of public service. As the City Council takes over new responsibilities in our new Kenya, the citizens of our capital City should work with and support their Council, in its efforts to make Nairobi a City of which the whole of Kenya can be proud.

A ND then on September the 6th, 1963, at a Hospital ceremony in Nairobi, the Prime Minister spoke of health services in terms of population mechanics and financial realities, and emphasized the need for local professional training:

I am very happy to have been invited here to perform this opening ceremony ... (Nurses' Training School and Home at The Aga Khan Platinum Jubilee Hospital in Nairobi) ....

You will be aware from the KANU Election Manifesto that it is our aim to move, as fast as the financial situation will permit, to the provision of free basic State health services.

The 1962 population census revealed that the population of Kenya is increasing at the rate of about three per cent. per annum, and this fact makes it difficult for the Government to keep pace with the growing demand for health services, let alone improve on the standards that have already been attained.

You will get some idea of the extent of the problem when I say that, merely to keep level with the population increase, it will be necessary to provide an additional 350 hospital beds each year, at a capital cost of about £280,000. To make an appreciable improvement in the ratio of beds to population, that figure should be doubled, and the additional recurrent commitment arising from capital expenditure on this scale is formidable. At the same time, to continue with our programme of rural health centres would require capital expenditure of at least £200,000 per annum.

I need hardly emphasize the importance of self-help in the provision of improved services, particularly in the matter of amenity beds and facilities, such as those provided at this fine Hospital. I am glad of this opportunity to pay tribute to Your Highness ... (The Aga Khan) ... and to the Ismaili community generally, for the admirable example which the community has constantly set in this respect.

At this important time in the history of Kenya, the need to accelerate training in all spheres and at all levels is paramount. As far as the Ministry of Health is concerned, there are plans to step up the tempo of training all round, including postgraduate training. Efforts are now being made to obtain financial assistance to establish an Institute for postgraduate training in Nairobi, which will be associated with the University of East Africa.

As regards undergraduate medical training, there will undoubtedly be a need for the establishment of a Medical School by 1967 or 1968. This will be an expensive undertaking, but it will be a necessity if Kenya is to achieve—within a reasonable period—a more satisfactory ratio of doctors to population.

In Kenya, the ratio of fully-trained nurses to population is about one per 8,000, from which it will be seen that—for many years to come—the country will be able to absorb as many trained nurses as can be produced from its training schools, now three in number. The qualification of Kenya Registered Nurse is equivalent to that of State Registered Nurse in Britain, and I hope that increasing numbers of girls of all races will decide to take up nursing as their profession.

PARTICULAR compassion for the plight of destitute children was revealed in the Prime Minister's speech—October the 24th, 1963—in Nairobi, when he opened an extension to a Children's Home:

I thank you for inviting me to open the new Nursery Wing of Thomas Barnardo House. It gives me the opportunity—which I readily and happily seize—of acknowledging in public the splendid work which Doctor Barnardo's Homes and the Kenya Committee have undertaken here in Nairobi, since General Sir Arthur Smith visited us three years ago.

I understand there is only one other Doctor Barnardo's Home outside Great Britain. I am glad indeed that we were able to persuade this world famous organization—which has done so much to bring hope and happiness into lives which before knew only anguish and despair—to come to our country to assist us in the task of caring for our own deprived children.

Today also gives me the opportunity to thank voluntary organizations generally for the splendid work they are doing in the field of social welfare. The Government has relied on them heavily in the past, and will certainly continue to rely on them heavily in the future. I want them to know that their presence in Kenya is greatly welcomed, and their invaluable work fully recognized.

It is a matter of great regret to my colleagues and myself that we are not always able to assist voluntary organizations, or to match their own financial contributions, to the extent that we would wish. This is because the demands which are made on our resources are enormous. The inability of the Government, however, to meet all these demands, does not excuse society from its duty to care and provide for the deprived, the hungry, the sick and the unwanted. It is here that the voluntary organizations today play such a vital part.

Here in this Home today are citizens of tomorrow. If we could open 50 similar Homes today, we could—alas!—fill them overnight. Let us not forget that those for whom no haven exists will also grow up to be citizens of tomorrow. But what kind of citizens are they likely to be, if they are brought up without love or faith, and in want and sickness? Ignorance, poverty and disease: here is the challenge which faces us today, which faces the Government and each individual member of society. I am sure we shall answer the challenge.

SOME months later—on June the 25th, 1964—Jomo Kenyatta was the central figure at a presentation ceremony, held on Wilson Airfield just outside Nairobi. On this occasion, he spoke reflectively of the meaning of 'health' and the contribution of science. And his conclusion was that social solutions were essential not just to the poorer countries, but for the stability and progress of all mankind:

We have come here today to witness the presentation of yet another aeroplane to the East African Flying Doctor Service, which is part of the East African Medical Research Foundation.

This Foundation makes an invaluable contribution to a wider and more comprehensive network, constituting the sum total of efforts—individual, private, voluntary and Government—to promote and maintain the health of the nation.

We live in a world where maladies, diseases and other health problems outstrip our present facilities and trained personnel. In the medical sphere, it is true to say that the term 'health' does not only mean the mere absence of disease and infirmity. It also implies a state of complete physical, mental and social wellbeing among the people. As such, things like food and housing have a direct bearing on the people's health.

From the point of view of our economic development alone, we know that malnutrition and disease cause low productivity of the workers. This low productivity itself maintains conditions of malnutrition and disease, which then cause even lower productivity and industrial strife. A way must be found to break this vicious circle in any developing country.

The active principle of science is discovery, the endless search for truth. This calls for acceptance of new theories until either they have ceased to have any meaning, or until newer ones have replaced them.

Our generation and the coming ones must therefore be prepared to reform and discard those old—and even modern—customs which are incompatible with progress, in order to facilitate the application of modern science to our problems. They must understand better the conditions and environments around them. They cannot afford to be narrow and naive, cynical and uncritical. They must make modest efforts in curiosity, as well as in the exercise of the intellect. This also applies—in a special sense—to those in the medical profession.

The African Medical Research Foundation is to be thanked and commended for its initiative and foresight, not only in conducting research, but also in helping our needy people in many isolated areas on numerous occasions.

Their own aircraft—and the aeroplanes they have chartered to meet emergencies—have gone out on mercy flights totalling over 250,000 miles. Flying surgeons have performed over 600 operations in remote parts of the country. They have also brought more than 200 people to Nairobi for specialist treatment.

The people themselves, under self-help schemes, have assisted by building airstrips at some of these distant hospitals, thus facilitating and speeding up these mercy flights.

Without the generous moral, financial and material support which the Foundation has received from friends and wellwishers in Kenya—and in Britain and America—this most useful work would have been stifled, or carried out so slowly as to diminish its value.

We thank these people for their noble form of benevolence. We also appreciate their realization that solution to health problems is not only essential to the developing countries, but also to the future wellbeing of the world.

THE role of women in nation building, and the fashioning of an essential partnership—based on mutual respect—between men and women, were other matters that the Prime Minister considered of importance in moving towards social reform. When opening the first East African Women's Seminar at Kabete, on April the 12th, 1964, he made these comments:

I would like to extend my hearty welcome to all participants in this first East African Women's Seminar.

After our victorious political revolution, we now owe it to ourselves to bring about a social and cultural revolution, within the framework of our present society. We have no illusions about the extent to which you—the women—have contributed towards the achievement of freedom, and the restoration of our full human stature and human dignity. Nor do we doubt your ability to make considerable contribution, in utilizing Africa's wealth for the betterment of our people and the advancement of our rich cultural heritage.

One of the greatest restraints to the natural growth of human beings—political inequality—has almost passed into history. The twin evils of coercion and exploitation, the oppression of nation State by nation State for selfish reasons, are fast disappearing from the face of the earth. We must, however, sustain our attacks on them so long as they exist.

Economically, much remains to be done. Approximately two-thirds of the world's wealth goes to less than one-third of the world's population. This minority is in the industrialized nations. It is our sacred duty to break the vicious circle of poverty by industrializing ourselves, by increasing exports, and by pressing forward with modern methods of increasing wealth.

While much progress has been made in these spheres, there is an urgent need for a thorough and objective examination of the relationship of men and women in the context of our social structure.

So far as you are concerned, you should first consider what you ought to see when you look ahead. This must be in terms of the best ways and means of promoting conditions, and attitudes of mind, which are conducive to progress. You should remember, however, that all that is modern is not necessarily progressive. Do not throw away those cultural values of old times which are inherently African. If you discard them now, they may be lost for ever.

On the other hand, the concept of partnership between men and women in society must be respected and be given practical application by both sexes. Men should understand that the future is as bright for women as it is for them. They should know that the employment of women in commerce and industry is not a threat to their security, but a long-term investment.

We recognize the fact—both urgent and important—that women should have equal access to education. Our planning at present, and in the future, will be so contrived as to arrange this. The importance of this cannot be over-emphasized. When women are educated and enlightened, then public opinion—measured as fact, belief and will—is invariably healthy and deeply ingrained. The importance of education in the home is lent great weight by the fact that it is there that children first learn something of human character and contrivance, of government on at least domestic scale.

I now ask you to tell the world what will be your role in harnessing our development in all these fields. I also exhort you to contemplate the happiness that awaits you, when all your faculties of mind and body shall be fully cultivated and developed.

THE remarks made by Mzee Kenyatta on that occasion, relating to the education of women, were not just polite observations. At Githunguri (October, 1964) he returned to this theme:

Under the sponsorship of the Christian Churches Educational Association, the school . . . (Githunguri Secondary School) . . . was this year permitted to operate as an unaided school for girls. This was certainly a most praiseworthy recognition of the need to foster girls' education. No people can go forward without their womenfolk being given a major and significant role to play.

A most particular interest of the Prime Minister, during this eighteen-month expanse, was the future of the country's youth. He recognized the contribution made by organizers and contingents of youth during the struggle for Uhuru. He understood the burning ambition, and even the dawning impatience, of youth. He saw the essential need for training and constructive opportunity, for outlets in which young men could exercise their energies and zest to serve the whole community, instead of being left in disillusionment, to drift—maybe—into a life of crime. At public rallies in Nairobi and Mombasa, many times, Jomo Kenyatta made some mention of this problem. He spoke of the plan for youth-training in each Region, on specially-acquired farms. He announced the enlistment of thousands of young men into the Army and the Police. He outlined new opportunities for youth in Government employment projects. Then one of his proudest moments came on October the 13th, 1964, when he presided at a Passing-out Parade, under the auspices of the National Youth Service, in Nairobi:

I salute you in the knowledge that you represent our nation's most important asset. The development of Kenya depends largely on the enthusiasm, courage and strength of our youth. Before these qualities can be used to the full, however, they must be strengthened with discipline and unity. The National Youth Service was formed to provide this, and—looking at you today—I am impressed by the quickness of your response. You have been in training for less than eight weeks, and your bearing and steadiness on parade does you and your instructors great credit.

As for unity, you have come from every part of Kenya. It makes me glad to see young representatives of every tribe and area standing shoulder to shoulder as brothers. This is an example to the country, and it must be followed in every aspect of our national life.

You have been trained as Junior Leaders, and you are about to be entrusted with a share of responsibility for the guidance of those thousands of young people who will follow you into the National Youth Service. You have the great task in front of you of helping to build good citizens, and of channelling the zeal and energy of youth into true nation building.

This task may take you into isolated parts of Kenya; it will mean hard work; there will be many difficulties that you must overcome. I know that I can rely on your courage and loyalty to overcome every obstacle, and that you will make the National Youth Service the spearhead of our struggle against ignorance, poverty and disease.

11

Security of the State

OF all the events in East Africa which sponsored world press headlines throughout this period, few were more electrifying than the military mutinies which broke out—and were quickly confined—in all three mainland territories. Some six weeks after Kenya's Independence, there was an outbreak here of mutinous conduct, involving some of the men of just one Battalion of the Kenya Army, at just one Camp. On January the 25th, 1964, speaking in Nairobi, the Prime Minister made a calm and factual statement:

Last night, there was an incident at Lanet Camp, arising out of an attempt by some soldiers of the 11th Battalion of the Kenya Army to defy authority. The action of these soldiers is a grave betrayal of the trust and confidence given to them by the Government and people of Kenya. Our Army has one of the best records and reputations in the world. They have my complete confidence, and I am sure that they enjoy also the confidence of all our people.

Our country and Government must be able to count on the men of the Kenya Army to protect and guarantee the sovereignty and integrity of our new nation. They must be the protectors of the peace of our country, and be counted upon to give support to the Police, if necessary, in maintaining law and order.

During the Colonial days, the men of the K.A.R. served the British Government loyally. Now that we have our own African Government, the world and our own people are justified in expecting even greater loyalty from the Kenya Army. I am sure that the Kenya Army will live up to this expectation. It would be unfair for anyone to try and use last night's incident for propaganda purposes, or to use it to discredit our Army generally.

Those who took part in the Lanet incident have gravely broken military discipline, and must be dealt with firmly. They will be dealt with according to military law. There will be no compromise on this, and I do not intend to meet them or to allow any of my Ministers to negotiate with them.

Only yesterday, I issued a statement announcing the decision of the Government, setting up a Committee to study conditions in the Army and to examine any genuine grievances. Through this Committee, the Government will listen carefully to any points brought forward by the Officers and men of the Kenya Army. The Committee will report to me on March the 1st, after which Government will decide the steps to be taken. In the same statement, I explained that we shall press on with the programme of Africanization in the Kenya Army, and I hope that most of the top Officer and executive posts will be held by Africans within this year.

The Government is also proud to have a Police force whose reputation and record is the envy of many other forces in the world. Here, too, Government is confident of the loyalty and the ability of the Police to maintain law and order throughout the country. The Government is conscious of the need for a contented Police force, and is working very rapidly in its programme of Africanization.

I must warn all our people most firmly, whether they be in the Army, Police, Youth Wings, Members of Parliament, or just members of the public, that the Government will deal most severely with any breaches of the peace or acts of disloyalty and destruction. You must remember that any violence or destruction can only harm our own people. We all have a duty to maintain the good name of Kenya, and I call upon everyone to accept his full part in this.

There is no reason for panic. We have taken sufficient precautionary measures to deal with any eventuality, but I am confident no action will be necessary. Anyone spreading rumours to cause alarm and despondency will be dealt with under the existing law. The public is warned not to listen to rumours, and to go about their business normally.

THEN, in a broadcast to the nation on April the 14th, 1964, Mzee Kenyatta followed up his earlier remarks about conditions of service, and announced some conclusions:

I am speaking to the soldiers of the Kenya Army, as well as to members of the Police and Prison services. I hope all citizens of Kenya will also listen to me.

On January the 24th, I announced the setting-up of a Committee to inquire into the Army grievances. Despite what I had said, a mutiny broke out at Lanet that same evening amongst soldiers of the 11th Kenya Rifles. Two hundred soldiers have been discharged from the Army, and some 70 are being tried according to military law.

One of the proudest moments of my life came on the day of our Independence, when the nation honoured the Army by giving our own soldiers the important task of lowering the British Flag and raising our own Flag in its place. The betterment of the Army, Police and Prisons services has been uppermost in my mind for more than 40 years.

Every effort is being made to form new units, so that those who have been in troubled areas can come out and have a well-earned rest. However, the formation of these new units depends to a certain extent upon what terms and conditions of service can be offered. The amount of money to be paid to a soldier, a policeman, or a member of the prison service, the amount of free food he can have, the free clothes, and the size and quality of his accommodation, depend upon the money we can afford, and must be related as nearly as possible to the general wage structure of the country.

The Committee which the Government set up to examine terms and conditions of service has made its report. This report has been considered and approved by my Government. The changes to the terms and conditions of service will be made known immediately, through normal channels. I should like everyone listening to me tonight to realize that your Government has given very serious thought to the pay and conditions of the uniformed services. Each one of us knows how important it is to have happy and contented security forces, but there is also the aspect of pride of service.

Each soldier, and policeman, and member of the prison service, is in a position of trust and responsibility towards the civilian population. It must also be remembered that our young country can ill afford luxury, and that in the armed forces as in other walks of life, Kenya needs some sacrifice from every citizen: aware that loyalty and service to our country, and devotion to duty, are more than money can buy.

The rates of pay which have been recommended compare favourably with those received by employees in commerce and industry, and when you remember the other free benefits given to the services, which have to be paid for out of earnings by the ordinary people, then the serviceman can indeed hold his head up high and be proud of his privileged position.

I hope that all members of the uniformed services, whatever their rank, will show to Kenya and to the world that the loyalty of our forces amply justifies the trust and confidence which we have placed upon them.

IN this last speech, the Prime Minister spoke of his pride that Kenya's own Army had been given honoured tasks throughout the country's Independence celebrations. Satisfaction at the increasingly-local command of the Kenya Army, and confidence in its patriotism, were constant themes. Following extracts are from speeches in Mombasa (February, 1964); Nairobi (June, 1964); and Nairobi (July, 1964):

We have an Army to clamp down on any trouble, and we are ready . . . . The significant thing is that the African Government, within a short time, has done more for the Army than the imperialists did in seventy years. We now have our Majors and Captains in the Army, and soon now our Forces will be commanded by an African . . . . At the same time, we are in the process of training African pilots.

* * *

We have no Monarchy, and so our Army—which used to be called the King's African Rifles—is now known as the Kenya Rifles . . . . Before we took over, there were only Effendis, but there are many African Officers now.

* * *

In the Army, we used only to have Effendis, who were not much more than watchmen. Yet today we have nearly 100 African Officers in our Army. There is an African Officer in charge of the troops who are fighting the shifta.

BUT no country can boast of a security pattern rooted in ground units alone. Thus, on the first anniversary of Internal Self-government, June the 1st, 1964, another of the Prime Minister's ambitions came to fruition, when he performed the Inauguration Ceremony of the new Kenya Air Force:

I have already announced measures to increase the numbers and the fire-power of our Army and Police. I am proud now to add yet another brick to our defence. Today, the Kenya Air Force is born.

I am very proud of the young men who stand before you today as our Air Force nucleus. I think you will agree with me that not many newly independent countries have been able to build up defence forces of our scale and standard.

I should like to reveal a secret, which was impossible before, during the previous régime. I sent some of these young men for training abroad, before the British left this country. We are grateful to the Government of Israel for receiving and training these pilots.

And now I want to express our appreciation to the British Government, which has undertaken to finalize the training of these young men. They have been generous in placing at our disposal the necessary aircraft and instructors.

To you young men, I would say this:

The country has placed upon you high hopes and expectations. Your task will be challenging, exciting and responsible. You are committed to serve this country, if necessary by laying down your lives, in the spirit of sacrifice of your own folk, some of whom are no longer with us. As a group of airmen, and part of our armed forces, we want you to set unrivalled standards of loyalty, efficiency, integrity and discipline. Above all, you are part of our society. You must respect other Kenyans who are less privileged than yourselves. In this way, you will build respect for yourselves and the country, in the true spirit of 'harambee'.

L ATER in the same month, during two further public speeches in Nairobi, he referred to this again:

There is no comparable indigenous Air Force in East Africa . . . . It is a healthy sign that those who were our exploiters yesterday have become reciprocal friends today.

* * *

We have already taken over Eastleigh Airport. Our own pilots are flying aircraft out of Eastleigh nowadays. We shall soon have fifteen of our own aircraft—not those small ones, but large planes which can be used against the shifta.

A PART altogether from national security in any military context, the Prime Minister was greatly conscious of the need for a proper Police establishment, and for high professional standards of Police operation. He constantly urged the requirement of mutual respect between the public and the Police, and at almost every public meeting he addressed he emphasized the vital importance—as the basis of stability—of law and order in the country. These quotations, respectively, are from speeches at Nairobi (June, 1964); Kamarin (January, 1964); Mombasa (February, 1964); Githunguri (September, 1964); and Loitokitok (February, 1964):

Police do not go about kicking people these days, because they are under my jurisdiction and I have told them to respect all citizens. Equally, you should respect the Police and co-operate with them. If you see thieves or robbers, do not hesitate to tell the Police.

* * *

I ask you to respect everyone in this country as your brothers, by keeping and maintaining law and order.

* * *

I must warn very strongly that the Government will deal firmly with anyone who attempts to break the law. Action of this kind will not be tolerated.

* * *

Unless people appreciate self-help, they tend to want to get things easily, and by dishonest means. This was not the way in the old days. Gikuyu did not possess a key at all: he left his house and his property open, and nobody touched a thing. Yet today there are people who would steal the hair from your head . . . . You should join with the Government and report all lawlessness—all robberies, thefts and murders—to the Police.

* * *

No country can survive unless law and order are maintained. Unconstitutional acts, irrational speeches, damage to life and property, can only undermine confidence in the stability of our country. Then, without capital coming into Kenya from other countries, there can be very little development. Without development, there can be no solution to unemployment, and living standards cannot be raised.

WHILE the Prime Minister roundly condemned lawbreakers of all kinds, he also devoted many passages to warning those who sought to undermine the country—or confidence in the country—by spreading rumours, by sowing dissension, or by subversion sponsored from somewhere outside. Examples of these warnings have been taken from speeches at Mombasa (February, 1964); Nairobi (June, 1964); in the National Assembly (July, 1963); at Nairobi (July, 1964); and a little later in Nairobi again:

There have been reports of people trying to sow the seeds of dissension. Instead of releasing their energies to reconstruct Kenya, these people go about trying to create confusion. To such people I would say: Since the beginning of the world, how many people have come and gone? All people come and go. So please do not spoil the world, because you will not live for ever. Try to live in peace, and leave the world a better place than you found it.

*   *   *

There are people who call themselves leaders, and who say they have no confidence in this Government. I must know whether or not you have confidence in your Government, and whether you have given these people any mandate to oppose the Government.

*   *   *

Anyone who wants to weaken this Government will be dealt with ruthlessly by the Government. We recognize the Opposition, but we cannot allow anyone to belittle this Government. This is not the Government of Nairobi, or Nakuru, or Kisumu, but the Government of Kenya, and the sooner the Opposition recognizes this the better.

*   *   *

There are those who keep going around saying 'this Government has not given us jobs'. Some of you are in fact being misled by trouble-makers, whose only interest is to see you in difficulties. My Government is a Government of action, and will not hesitate to deal with these few trouble-makers in the country . . . .We have gained a good reputation in the world, and throughout Asia and Africa; but there are still a few people here who want to spoil our good name abroad.

*   *   *

I must warn these people . . . (those who took bribes from foreigners in order to cause confusion in the country) . . . that the Government is fully aware of their activities, and a full scale investigation is going on. I will deal with them very firmly when they are known.

THE Prime Minister took a personal hand, more than once, to help responsible Ministers in their efforts to rehabilitate forest fighters—following an amnesty—and to stop any outbreaks of oathing in certain parts of Kenya. In August, 1964, during a tour, Jomo Kenyatta made these points, first at Chuka and then at Kigaari:

There are people who go about telling others to return to the forests. These people who go into the forests and feed on stolen things, are they not vagabonds? . . . We took oaths to regain our freedom. But if people ask you to take oaths now, it will be oaths against your Government, and therefore against yourselves . . . Recently, I ordered that all freedom fighters who were in prison should be released. I then said there was going to be an amnesty, and I asked the Minister to set aside about 400 farms. But these one-time forest fighters, offered all these things, said they preferred the Army. If these people now refuse to co-operate, and go into the forests, will you pity them and help them again?

*   *   *

Oath-taking must stop, since there is no longer any need for this. Neither is there further need for making guns, as we now possess all the modern guns in this country. All soldiers are our soldiers.

AT the same time, the Prime Minister recognized that there were still outstanding grievances. He made it clear that these—in many cases—could and should be redressed. But he insisted, at all times, that justice could only be approached through the administrative channels laid down by the African Government, and due processes of law. At Githunguri in September, 1964, he summed up basic issues:

Any land that was confiscated during the Emergency has been recorded in the Lands Office. Those who had their land taken away will eventually get it back—but this cannot happen overnight.

*   *   *

Channels are still open for rectification of injustices committed in the process of land consolidation. Those who have genuine grievances have recourse to courts of law. But there is one important thing: please examine your facts. If you lose your case, it is no good saying you have been swindled.

12

Leadership knows no Respite

CONSTITUTIONAL reform, African unity, foreign affairs, the agrarian revolution, economic development, education and social welfare, internal and external security . . . . all these and many other vital or complex issues received, during this expanse of time, the Prime Minister's personal touch. In this concluding Chapter, examples will be given—beyond or within these basic headings—of the elastic scope of those responsibilities and duties and interests which became attached, as well, to the leader of the Kenya nation. As a first instance, it was Mzee Jomo Kenyatta, speaking in Parliament on July the 30th, 1963, who launched Kenya's National Fund:

With the approach of Independence, the time has arrived for the people of Kenya to show that they are prepared to help themselves in the spirit of 'harambee'. One of the most practical ways in which we can do this is by establishing a National Fund, to which all can contribute for development of the country.

Such a National Fund will be established to mobilize contributions from farmers, traders, industrialists and citizens from all walks of life, who wish to celebrate Independence in a meaningful way by making a much-needed contribution to the development of Kenya.

It is fitting that the Fund should be used to finance projects which will glorify the Kenya nation. Thus, it would be proper to use the Fund to help finance the building which will house this National Assembly, which embodies our belief in democracy and nationhood.

Secondly, a Fund which has received contributions from the people should itself be of direct benefit to the people, and we intend that it shall be. For example, the Fund will be used to assist those who are embarking on self-help schemes. It will also help the people of Kenya by providing money for education, health and other social purposes.

The people of Kenya are all out for the improvement and development of their country. In order to achieve this, we must be ready to help ourselves. The National Fund will provide visible proof that Kenya can help and develop itself. It will be a demonstration to the world that, when we say Kenya will be a great nation, we mean it, and we mean to do something to accomplish it.

THEN on May the 29th, 1964, to meet distress caused by renewed flooding in various parts of Kenya, Mzee Kenyatta launched a more specific Appeal Fund:

The Government has had to face a number of natural disasters at various times. The last one occurred in 1961, when people were afflicted by flooding in Nyanza, Coast, Ukambani and Masai areas. In the past few weeks, we have had serious flooding in the Nyanza and Western Regions, and to a less extent in the Coast Region.

Every time we have suffered such disasters, the Government has had to resort to the normal Famine Relief Fund, which is never sufficient to deal adequately with the situation. So we have only managed to help those in need through generous assistance. It is very gratifying that the public has in fact donated generously, and voluntary agencies in this country and abroad have all played a prominent part.

It has become very clear, however, that *ad hoc* measures to deal with these disasters have not been entirely adequate. I have therefore decided to launch a National Disaster Relief Fund, so that every individual and organization can have an opportunity to contribute. This will ensure that—in the event of some new disaster occurring—there will be something readily available.

The spirit of 'harambee' has been abundantly demonstrated by many citizens and organizations during the present flooding in Nyanza and Western Regions. I now appeal to everyone to give generously, in a neighbourly spirit, knowing that our efforts towards nation building will be worth little if some of our people continue in misery and hardship as a result of natural catastrophe.

★

IN quite a different field, when the new broadcasting service was inaugurated— as 'The Voice of Kenya'—on July the 1st, 1964, it was the Prime Minister who delivered, on the radio and television networks, an explanatory address:

I am proud to be here tonight to join my countrymen in rejoicing over the inauguration of the 'Voice of Kenya'. This is a great occasion in the history of broadcasting in our country, and constitutes a major decision taken since we freed ourselves from the chains of Colonialism. Up till last night, as you all know, this vital medium of information was not under the direct control of our Government. We are proud that from now on it will serve us unhampered by outside interests or pressures.

Radio broadcasting was started in Kenya in 1928, by a private Company. The original programmes were in English only, but during the Second World War these were extended to include Asian broadcasts. It was at this time that the Government also introduced a small broadcasting service—information and news—designed to reach African askaris. As you may know, this African Broadcasting Service become a part of the Government Information Department, while the English and Asian language programmes continued under the management of Messrs. Cable & Wireless.

In 1959, these three services were combined and became one Government Department, called the Kenya Broadcasting Service. This Department existed until 1961, when it was decided that broadcasting should be run by an independent Corporation. This was the birth of the K.B.C., which functioned until midnight yesterday. The decision to nationalize the K.B.C. is one which my Government has not taken lightly.

You are aware that radio and television are powerful weapons; if they are not properly controlled, they can be used to destroy a nation. We in Kenya are determined that these media will be employed to build our unity, to keep the people well informed, educated and entertained. Obviously, these services cannot be effective unless they are properly supervized, and given regular and adequate financial support. It is a sad thing that, during the past twelve months, the K.B.C. has been faced with immense financial problems, and I regret that when it was created sufficient care was not taken to ensure that the Corporation would have enough working capital to enable it to carry on without being involved in heavy debt.

As you know, a Commission of Inquiry was appointed, and came to the conclusion that broadcasting in Kenya should be controlled by Government, in order to justify the substantial payments which the service was now receiving from the Exchequer. We accepted the Commission's recommendation. Parliament has supported the Government fully on this matter, and the take-over of the K.B.C. has now become effective.

I wish to assure the country that the 'Voice of Kenya' will reflect the divergent views of the nation as a whole. Obviously, we will use it to popularize Government policies and programmes. The Opposition, too, if they have something interesting and constructive to say, will be free to use these facilities. We also expect that leaders from other walks of life will use them. In other words, we expect the 'Voice of Kenya' to become a forum for the free expression of opinion by the peoples of this country.

Nevertheless, I would like to emphasize that this privilege must not be abused. The 'Voice of Kenya' must not be used to undermine the Government or any of Kenya's friends, or to work against any individual leader or citizen, or section of our society.

It is our intention to produce more local films, so that the Kenya television service can reflect a true image of our cultural heritage. And we expect to implement plans for the launching of external broadcasting, so that the 'Voice of Kenya' can be heard far beyond our borders.

Before concluding, I have a special tribute to pay to the broadcasting staff for their hard work during a most trying period. Were it not for their loyalty and diligence to duty, it would not have been possible for the broadcasting service to achieve the high degree of technical efficiency which we all witness.

★

ONE of the most vivid examples of the Prime Minister's force of personality, his ability to transmit convictions, instil loyalty, and transform past suspicions into future inspiration, was heard at a meeting in Nakuru on August the 12th, 1963. There, some hundreds of European farmers and their wives were assembled. It was an expectant scene, in a Town Hall that—through the years —had known many stormy meetings, at a time when 'winds of change' were taking shape. Jomo Kenyatta just walked to the front of the stage. He leaned on his stick, talking quietly at first, then his voice gathered strength. He talked farming, to an audience of farmers. He made some careful declarations, and gathered up the fears and apprehensions of these people, and set their minds at ease. He cracked some jokes. And at the end, this European concourse all rose up to their feet, joining him in cries of HARAMBEE! Lord Delamere called this a unique and historic occasion. These were a few of the Prime Minister's remarks:

We want you to stay and to farm well in this country: that is the policy of this Government . . . . What the Government needs is experience, and I don't care where it comes from: I will take it with both hands . . . . Continue to farm your land well, and you will get all the encouragement and protection of the Government. The only thing we will not tolerate is wasted land . . . . Kenya is large enough, and its potential is great. We can all work together harmoniously to make this country great, and to show other countries in the world that different racial groups can live and work together.

MZEE Kenyatta made frequent reference to relationships between the new African Government and members of other races, and emphasized that there would be no discrimination between citizens of the Kenya nation. In the National Assembly (July, 1963), and at Githunguri (September, 1964), he said:

In our KANU manifesto, we stated clearly that we were not going to discriminate because of race, colour or religion. We are going to treat Kenyans on an equal footing, and the law of Kenya is going to apply equally to all European, Asian and African citizens of this country.

*   *   *

Speaking as the leader of my Party, I would like to pose this question: when we were fighting for freedom and human dignity, how many non-Africans died in this struggle? The non-Africans must abandon their old strategy. They must realize this was consigned to the flames, with all other vestiges of imperialism, on Independence Day. We do not want such people to change their colour. To them I simply say: turn and become Africans in your hearts, and we will welcome you with open arms.

OCCASIONALLY, the Prime Minister found it necessary to relate his remarks to those of Asian origin. At Mombasa in July of 1963 (first quotation, below) he uttered words of encouragement to a gathering of Asian businessmen, but then in Nairobi in June of 1964 there were words of warning:

The Government is not just a KANU Government, but the Government for every citizen of Kenya. Irrespective of what race or religion you belong to, we will work for you all . . . . We want to retain your skills and business experience, and wish you to continue to work as you have done in the Colonial days.

*   *   *

Indians must learn as well, and must adapt themselves to live with our people. They must obey the African rule.

I say that if there are any Asians who are unwilling to work with us, they can pack their bags and go.

THE thinking behind the Government's policy on Africanization was clearly conveyed in the Kenyatta Day speech with which this volume began. In fact, the Prime Minister set the stage for this policy in one of his earlier speeches (July the 23rd, 1963) in the House of Representatives:

It is the policy of this Government to Africanize the Civil Service as quickly as we can. But at the same time, what we need to remember is not the colour of a person's skin, nor anyone's race. We want experienced people. Some of these people—whom my friends regard as imperialists or colonialists—have experience which we need. Until we train our people to hold these posts, we cannot—in a day, as soon as we achieve Independence—scrap every post and say we will put black men in them because they are black.

In my Government, I want experience, and I do not care where I get it. Unless we have a Government with capable Officers to run it, then our Government will fall. I want the people to understand this: that we have this policy of Africanization, that people are being trained for various posts, and that when they are ready we shall give them responsibility. But we cannot take people just because they are black.

THAT the Prime Minister was gratified by progress could be discerned (June, 1964) at a public rally in Nairobi:

We promised that independence would mean greater responsibilities for our people. We now have African Civil Secretaries and Regional Government Agents. In the Government Departments, we have done away with imperialists. All the main responsible jobs are now held by Africans.

THEN, at a news conference on September the 16th, 1964, the Prime Minister combined an important Africanization announcement with a renewed assurance to expatriate Officers in the Public Service:

The Government—after careful consultation with the Chairman of the Police Service Commission and Sir Richard Catling—has decided that Sir Richard's place as Inspector-General of Police will be taken by an African Officer on January the 1st next. Sir Richard's retirement is no reflection on the admirable service he has rendered to the Government of Kenya prior to and after Independence.

The decision is in accord with the Government's policy for the Africanization of the Public Service.

I am glad of this opportunity to say again that the work being done by expatriate Officers still in the Service is valuable and appreciated. I wish also to assure them that, until such time as they can be replaced by Africans, their services will continue to be required, and they need fear no victimization.

★

ANOTHER problem ... Masailand. This was commonly presented as a 'problem' at some of the initial constitutional Conferences, on the strength of statutory provisions made in the years 1904 and 1911, and because the development of this large area of southern Kenya presented some special difficulties. The Prime Minister—familiar with the area—took a personal interest in the complexities and needs of Masailand. During discussion in Nairobi with a delegation of 80 Masai leaders, on September the 20th, 1963, he declared:

I want the Masai people to understand clearly that there is no one at all—including the Government—who will take the Masai land. Our aim is to protect you and help you to progress .... If the Masai people work with the Government, then within a few years the Masai country could be as good as any.

SUBSEQUENTLY, on visits to a number of centres in Masailand, the Prime Minister delivered assurances, presented opportunities, and offered advice. The following are extracts from speeches at Loitokitok (February, 1964); Kajiado (June, 1964) and Narok (June, 1964):

Remember that we are in the twentieth century, that we must move with the present-day times, and that throughout the world rapid changes are taking place in order that progress can be made for the betterment and help of all people.

In this spirit, I ask you to keep good cattle rather than over-stocking. This overstocking can only cause soil erosion, and scarcity of food for all of you. By keeping good cattle and not overstocking, and by taking an interest in agriculture where good crops can be grown, it will be easier for all of you to progress in every way.

I realize that many of your difficulties spring from inadequate supplies of water to many areas. I can assure you that the Government will try its level best, with all the means in its power, to look into this very acute problem. The need for the provision of adequate water supplies in the Masai country is fully recognized. However, it is not possible always to provide a free supply of water. Drilling and equipping boreholes, and constructing water pipelines, are expensive operations, and for these reasons charges may have to be made for water supplied.

*   *   *

I am aware that the Masai have special problems. The Colonialists did not do much to help the Masai. They just left them like game, for people to come and take their pictures.

*   *   *

Nobody is going to touch Masailand. It will remain for the Masai. It is in black-and-white in the Constitution that Masailand will not be taken by anyone else.

Since you have land, you must develop it. God has given you good land and good soil. If you co-operate with the Government, we shall help you to get machines to cultivate the land to grow good crops. We shall help you to improve your livestock. The Government will help you to get water.

There is £1½ million available for development in Masailand. You will have that money if you co-operate with the Government. The Masai should realize from this assistance that we now have an African Government, not a Colonial régime.

In the old days, the sign of ability was a spear and a shield. Today, it is the exercise book and the pen. We do not govern today with spears and shields. The pen is many times mightier than the sword. The Masai will gain high places in the Government if they become educated. If you have children ready for higher education overseas, bring them to us.

IT was appropriate that, while in the Masai areas, the Prime Minister should make specific references to wildlife conservation. The first quotation below is from his Loitokitok speech, which echoed views he had expressed in the House on August the 1st, 1963:

In the Masai country are very important tourist areas—the Amboseli and Mara Game Reserves. You all know the importance to the County Councils, and indeed to the whole of Kenya, of the tourist industry, which can draw in such vitally-needed revenue from overseas visitors. To maintain this, the Government needs your help and co-operation, in order that we can improve and make the Amboseli and Keekorok Lodges very attractive to our overseas visitors. The revenue from these will be very beneficial to the Kajiado and Narok County Councils.

Do everything in your power to preserve the wildlife in these areas. If you destroy that wildlife, you will also destroy one of the mainstays of the economy of our country. I ask you all to help in this matter.

* * *

Kenya's wildlife is one of the most important aspects of our economy, and we must take great care of wild animals. The Government is determined to protect wild game. This is something in which everyone should take an interest: the conservation of a national asset.

APRIL the 30th, 1964, was celebrated in Kenya as Tree Planting Day, and at a ceremony in the Uhuru Stadium, Mzee Kenyatta made these remarks:

We are today celebrating our first National Tree Planting Day, by planting a Mugumo tree . . . . The importance of trees was recognized by our forefathers for many reasons. Through trees and plants of all kinds, men of old perceived the wonders of nature, the wonders of creation . . . . Now, the preservation of forests is essential for the conservation of water, and the maintenance of the climatic and physical conditions of our country . . . . And as the demand for timber, fuel, paper and other goods increases, great care should be taken to plant more trees relatively to those which have been cut.

★

A ND so it went on. There was virtually no subject within the orbit of man's inquiry or objection that the Prime Minister was not asked to describe or rectify, to deal with or explain. This called for many sudden asides of wit or wisdom. For example (September, 1964, at Machakos), a comment on witchcraft:

If you see a witch doctor, you will invariably find that he is poor. If he says he will make you rich, ask why he is not rich himself.

E LSEWHERE, reflection on the ladies:

Of course, the world cannot exist without ladies. They are an important species.

A ND during the State Banquet (June, 1964) for the Emperor Haile Selassie, a well-received quip:

I would like to express our thanks to Your Majesty for the great honours which you have so graciously conferred upon us. The only slight difficulty which I foresee is where to place so many Grand Cordons of the Order of the Star of Honour, when our Table of Precedent comes to be revised!

★

S O ends this contemporary record, on the evidence of his own declarations and philosophies, of Mzee Jomo Kenyatta: the first and only Prime Minister of the independent Kenya nation; first President of the Kenya Republic.

As one of the leading figures on the present world stage, many have assessed his statesmanship, have found new hope in the dominance of his personality. His energy—in work and travel and fulfilling all public engagements—has become a legend.

His dedication was always directed to the sanctity of freedom, to the building of Kenya, to the ideals of pan-Africanism, to the fashion and the contribution of Africa's place in the world. In these causes, he exerted all his strength, and his work is not yet done.

But beneath this strength, apparent always to his closest colleagues and advisers, often glimpsed in the course of some duty, lies the motive of compassion, the gift of patience, the perspective of an elder statesman, the readiness always to be gay.

This, indeed, is an incomparable man.

Postscript

Since the main bulk of the manuscript of this book was delivered to the printers, in early November, 1964, the Opposition Party in the Legislature—KADU—has been voluntarily dissolved.

The Leader of the Opposition, Ronald Ngala, announced on November the 10th that all members of his Parliamentary Group would henceforth work with the Government. He reaffirmed that at no time had KADU opposed the formation of a Republic. Their opposition to the Republican Constitution had been on grounds of detail and on questions of decentralization. But it had become clear—as Ngala put it—that the country had chosen to enter the Republic under the one political leadership of Mzee Kenyatta. The Opposition would therefore bow to the popular will, and join the Government to work for future development in a spirit of national unity.

On that same day, the Bill embodying the Republican Constitution —passed earlier with more than the requisite majority by the House of Representatives—was unanimously approved by the Senate.

In a short statement to both Houses in turn, Mzee Kenyatta expressed his great satisfaction that differences and divisions of the past had now given way to political unity, so that all talents and energies and loyalties could henceforth be directed to the challenge of nation building.

The implication of all this was that Kenya would become a Republic by unanimous desire; that the Constitution—accepted by all—would give clear expression to national unity; that the Central Government would be in exclusive command of all vital policies and programmes; that national leadership would take a form which the people could readily understand; and that Parliament, in which there would be full opportunity for debate and demur, but without any obligatory opposition, would remain supreme.